To those of us who dare to look towards the future . . . .
Sometimes when the world seems to be falling apart,
it is simply restructuring. Restructuring a miraculous new
horizon just awaiting our participation.

Books by Eva Herr

Agape: The Intent of the Soul

CONSCIOUSNESS

Bridging the Gap Between
Conventional Science
and the New Super Science
of Quantum Mechanics

EVA HERR

RAINBOW RIDGE
BOOKS

Cover and interior design by Frame25 Productions
Cover photograph © Davi Sales Batista c/o Shutterstock.com

Published by:
Rainbow Ridge Books, LLC
140 Rainbow Ridge Road
Faber, Virginia 22938
434-361-1723

If you are unable to order this book from your local
bookseller, you may order directly from the distributor.

Square One Publishers, Inc.
115 Herricks Road
Garden City Park, NY 11040
Phone: (516) 535-2010
Fax: (516) 535-2014
Toll-free: 877-900-BOOK

Library of Congress Catalog Card Number applied for.

ISBN 1-937907-05-1

10 9 8 7 6 5 4 3 2 1

Printed on acid-free paper in the United States of America.

Contents

FOREWORD

Joyce A. Kovelman, Ph.D.

Joyce A, Kovelman is a neuroscientist, psychologist, personal coach, patient advocate, and ECOSOC representative to the United Nations on behalf of the University of Global Education.

IT IS TRULY A JOY to write the foreword to Eva Herr's remarkable new book on consciousness.

As most of Eva's readers know, Eva grew up in a Southern Baptist family, later converted to Orthodox Judiasm, and when her second marriage ended, she experienced an intense "dark night of the soul," that led her to deeply question reality as she presently understood it. Her beloved father had died during this period of time, and Eva never got to say good-bye nor tell her father how much she loved and missed him. One night, Eva had an amazing dream in which she visited with her father in another realm of awareness. There he presented her with lots of information, as well as a greater understanding of consciousness, reality, and the ground of being that each of us share with one another, for ALL are part of the One.

When Eva awakened, the "dark night of the soul" had lifted and she was filled with a desire to understand the incredible gift of information her father had shared with her, a yearning to know still more, and a need to find tangible scientific evidence that what she had suddenly and inexplicably learned is true. And so Eva's journey into the hidden, invisible "ground of being" began, leading her to still more discoveries and to others, who like her, didn't shy away from the puzzling, the strange, the unexplained, and the challenging new findings posed to them in their research, their classrooms, their laboratories, and their lives. Eva and the scholars she interviews in this book bravely risked ridicule, ostracism, and criticism when they stepped out of the box of conventional science and chose to further explore the findings and implications about this little known, non-physical universe that gives rise to our world. Somehow, like Alice in Wonderland, each of them had entered a profoundly different reality and science than most of us ever dream of.

Eva interviews some of the most brilliant, creative, and visionary scientists, philosophers, physicists, and critical thinkers in our world, all with impeccable credentials and truly remarkable accomplishments. Eva courageously asks those willing to share their ideas with her to take her readers along with her on a journey of discovery that few traditional and conventional scientists dare to take. She bravely and intelligently asks questions such as the nature of consciousness, the differences between mind and brain, energy versus physical objects, as well as the nature of body and soul. Eva is seeking answers from each of them to the hard and intriguing questions most of us know little about. Each person Eva interviews reveals the importance, as well as the necessity of paying attention to our subjective, inner experiences in order to more effectively relate and interact with the present world in which we live. Every one of the people interviewed by Eva offer us a new understanding and perception of the self, the world, and the cosmos, as well as a more hopeful understanding of reality at its most fundamental level.

There is remarkable agreement among those interviewed by Eva that consciousness always partners with energy, thereby allowing the passive flow of information to transform itself into intended action. Unless the two work as one, nothing can change or happen in our universe. Unless consciousness and energy travel together, we would have no past and no future, and find ourselves living in a static, meaningless cosmos. And though we still do not know what consciousness is, we learn that it is indeed possible to intentionally engage and affect consciousness and our own personal physical reality on many different levels. What Eva and these extraordinary interviews tell us, is that each of us has the ability to create a more satisfying and fulfilling life than we presently experience. In so doing, we gain clarity and the ability to share in vastly more rarified realms of being, and to grow in understanding and wisdom.

I wish to acknowledge the long journey of study and investigation that Eva has been on since receiving the profound gifts her father so lovingly bestowed upon her. In her interviews, Eva carefully frames and poses the questions she asks each person. She has done her homework and is well prepared. It's also heartwarming to note the frequent complements Eva receives regarding her questions, as well as the correctness of her comments. I felt all of these brilliant scholars showed respect for Eva's own level of consciousness, abilities, and discernment. Thus, you will find Eva's interviews are fluid and invite all of us into the discussion that unfolds. At times during these interviews, I no longer experienced myself as a reader. Instead, I felt as if I were included in the exchange of ideas, eager to ask questions of my own, and to join the fascinating and intriguing exploration of so many new and provocative ideas.

Remembering that each journey begins with the first step taken, I invite all of you to read this important and provocative book that offers us new ideas, a new science and a new vision of reality. *Consciousness* by Eva Herr calls out to all of humanity, inviting us to explore the hidden, invisible dimensions of existence and personhood, as well as to accept the gifts along with the responsibilities that come with awakening to a more challenging, mysterious universe. In so doing, we will begin to make wiser decisions, more appropriate choices, and take the necessary actions to accomplish the many things we feel called to do in the physical world. Let us make it so.

"*The happiness and greatness, the rank and station, the pleasure and peace of an individual has never consisted in his earthly wealth, but rather in his excellent character, his high resolve, the breadth of his learning and in his ability to solve problems.*"

—"Baha'u'llah," 1863

PREFACE

Stanislav Gergre O'Jack, Ph.D.

Stanislav Gergre O'Jack is a clinical psychologist with an emphasis in family systems, a licensed handicap counselor, a certified mediator, advisory board member and UN representative for the PRIDE organization (Pacific Rim Institute for Development and Education), and has a professional and academic background in mechanical engineering, architecture and design, and industrial design. He also conducts Subtle Energy research with physicists.

THE ENSUING SHARED INFORMATION, adroitly defined, presented by all of the interviewees in response to Eva Herr's insightful questions contained herein has catalyzed within me, in analogous form, an awe, in that I feel like an African or Chinese or Australian or Central American Aborigine that has been handed a "Smart-Phone"—a device or means with which one can access a near infinite volume of information. And thus, I am, in degrees, somewhat stunned in how to adjust to such scientific-theoretical-spiritual-accessible data. The one thought that I have as related to the following quotation is that I need to change my own present reference schema to:

"Free thyself from the fetters of this world, loose thy soul from the prison of self, seize thy chance for it will come to thee no more."
—"Hidden Words," Mirza Husayn Ali, 1863

Thus, as derived from the above quotations, all problems and difficulties presented to an individual—or to all of humankind on this plane of existence—evidently are signs of growth, in that all problems and difficulties are literally "*asking questions*" which most often lead to acceptable and coherent answers, which then guides our species to its next stage of development, ascending from conception to birth to childhood to pubescence and to adolescence—so that world peace will become a reality.

More than a mere human being who is seeking answers, it is the questions themselves that are seeking or demanding an answer for solutions to existing needs, and this book is based on *questions*, ones girded by the shared and clearly expressed *answers* or responses to them—to the degree humanly possible—as delineated by some of humankind's current astute minds. This is a book written and assembled by Eva Herr, a person who, with humility, states that she has a "scant" formal education.

Although seemingly the question responding individuals are replying with an objective posture, any and all statements ultimately are subjective as prefaced by the statement often stated, "This is my interpretation". . ."as based on past, present, and projected future knowledge." Thus, everything must begin with a question, which is the basis for Eva Herr's manuscript; it is tantamount to being a "*wake-up-call*" on behalf of all humankind.

Additionally, in keeping with Neils Bohr's concept of "complimentarity"—conceived and expressed circa 1932, or in Dr. Lazlo's mention of the ancient concept or reality of "yin yang" as found in Chapter 7— "if there is a proposed question, either outwards or inwards, then its complimentarity must be an answer," one to be found somewhere in the "entanglement of all" as often expressed by several interviewees. A question conceivably is an answer in itself, and if so, therefore, it is its own complimentarity, the latter in the sense that it identifies the existence of an unknown which elicits or provokes the yet-unknown to be "discovered, uncovered, identified or invented."

From my perspective, all questions of and all answers to anything and everything, although seemingly are based objectively within the limited and fleeting five-senses-realm per the existing basic scientific paradigm, are ultimately subjectively derived and subjectively expressed, and subjectively either agreed upon, denounced, challenge, or protracted.

Eva has assembled predominately a list of questions that seek answers regarding the nature of and the issue to the meaning of *"consciousness," "awareness,"* and *"intentionality."*

If one is *"conscious"* (e.g., sensory system) of his or her *"awareness"* (e.g., non-sensory system) of something, then how are they one and the same? Does it have to do with past and current misinterpretation of the words, and if so, why? Is someone *conscious* of their *awareness* or *aware* of their *consciousness*? For the present, other than the suggestion that *"intent"* follows *knowledge* and precedes *volition and action*, I will not comment further on *"intentionality."* "What, if any, is the difference between brain and mind?" Eva Herr repeatedly asks of every interviewee.

The answers either ranged from "the brain is all there is" and the "mind and brain are one and the same"—as put forth by the behaviorists in psychology beginning in the early 1900s, and in their model that "those who imply that the mind differs from the brain should not be argued with, since the mind is not to be clearly nor unambiguously defined anyway, so let us just talk about what to do with all of humankind's behavior as applied in a practical manner to the well-being of our species." (A similar venue-response by Dr. Tiller is in Chapter 5 regarding consciousness and awareness.) The latter can be juxtaposed to the Humanistic Psychology movement in the late 1960s, and also later when spirituality was introduced with aspects of "intuition," circa 1970-80, as proposed by Transpersonal Psychology. These were meant to restore and to remind people at large that the word *"psychology"* literally means the *study of the soul*, that the mind is non-physical, and that it, the ephemeral-like mind, functions *through* the brain, which is an element of the world of five senses, and that the mind does so via the papilla of the physical heart as transmitted through the fourth thorax of the spine—the heart chakra venue. (Persian Mystic 'Abdu'l-Baha, early 1900s).

So *telepathy*—conceivably a "short-cut" for transferring data—is put forth as a *mind-to-mind transfer* of information, whereas speech and vocabulary serve as sensory-means of information distribution. It is stated in ancient Islamic folklore that "the longest distance in the world is from the mind to the heart and the shortest distance is from the heart to the mind." Thus, telepathy in this non-physical paradigm is mind-to-mind, as it aborts or side-steps the complications of the mind-to-brain-to-brain-to-mind process of conveying information. In a "sense" *cell phones* are a form of *telepathy* in that one can talk into a small "box-like-thing" and obtain the "telepathic voice" transmitted from a distant person.

Mind-to-mind in the above schema differs from the behaviorist's model of brain-to-brain, since language does not exist in the mind-to-mind paradigm. It is a transfer or sharing of "unmitigated thought." As an example of how it is at times difficult to clearly convey a message between two languages, I will share an experience that I had in China in 1991 during a tour-bus excursion. The guide asked of me, "Why in the United States do you drive your car in the parkway and then park your car in the driveway?" In the English language "up" has over sixty applications, and there are numerous other words that look alike, sound alike, are spelled the same, or spelled differently although pronounced the same: "You mean, I am mean compared to the mean-average mean?" Perhaps mind-to-mind (thought to thought) best be explored more acutely.

The main question appears to be does the brain invent or merely record and distribute what the mind expresses via the sensory system (audible and written languages driven by logic), or does the mind dispense information through the aegis of a non-sensory system such as intuition, telepathy, and/or a great psychic guess?

In a book entitled *The Reality of Man,* it is suggested that there are two kinds of thought: one both begins and ends with thought (the manipulation of information) and the other begins with thought and ends with action. Also, the author of the above named book proposes that just as the sensory system (brain-body) has five senses, the non-sensory system also has five non-sensory aspects: *"Thinking"* (the manipulation of information wherein information could be defined as Data's Bits and Bytes), *"Comprehension"* (understanding of information), *"Memory"* (imprinting or information-storage), *"Knowledge"* (is information), and *"The Common Faculty"* (transmits information from the mind to the brain).

To further employ the computer and its components as a "logical" analogy to the human system, then the computer's main-frame is the brain, and that which controls the computer is the programmer (mind). The mind is an aspect of the soul. "The Common Faculty" of the soul is tantamount to being a *router* that sends messages to various parts of the brain—to its icons stored in different locations of the brain—with which to temporarily (physical life) store information to be used for different functions of the human body as clearly stated in current medical models which demonstrate that different parts of the brain contain information for biochemical functions, physical movement, language employment, food processing, eliminations, etc. In this new schema, logic and intuition—the higher part of the overall human system—are the basis for creativity, invention, and intervention, whereas the *ego is a rote response system* which assures the physical function of the human body.

To repeat: repetition "imprints" as is often said. Eva Herr continually addresses the issue of "what is consciousness" and what is "awareness" and are they one and the same? Is one conscious of their awareness of issues or is one aware of one's conscious state-of-being at all given times, or just during some fleeting moments?

Throughout the Introduction of this manuscript by Eva, regarding her purpose for creating this book, and within the interview chapters, what is apparently being put forth in context is that our species, Homo sapiens, is advancing intellectually, scientifically, philosophically, and spiritually, and therefore, there currently exists a variety and mix of differing "minds." Propitiously, in some Far East writings (of the Baha'i Faith) is a proverb that states, "From the clash of differing opinions often is ignited the spark of truth."

As predicated on the *"concept"* or *"reality"* that there is such a thing as God— "The Complimentary of all living/existing things throughout the Infinite Universe," whatever infinite means—then it certainly would have been great to have asked all the above questions of God through Its Physical Presence—*The Prophet* of all religions. Perhaps we best be prepared in advance for the "Next Return" with a list of questions for science, religion, and philosophy? I recall the time when my daughter was ten years old and my son was eight years old, and they were arguing who had the greatest number of something or another, and I decided to explain to them the concept of *infinity* in order to settle the argument. The next thing I heard from my daughter and son in their argument was, "I have infinity plus one," and my son replied to his sister that "he had infinity plus two." Thus, is this where our species may be today in respect to all of the above? The words, theme, and dedication of all the interviewees in Eva Herr's new book brings to mind the following prayer, a special message to all members of our species. I *"feel"* that the prayer reflects the theme and character of the interviewer and of all the individuals interviewed.

"O God! Make me as a teacher in Thy Cause. Cause my mouth to utter the wisdom of Thy ways. Make me wise, kind, good and understanding. Give me the courage of Thy Martyrs, the patience of Thy Saints and the knowledge of Thy Chosen Ones. Make me a fire that will burn through the darkness of men's ignorance, a flag that will fly above his weakness, and a song that will sing and echo through his despair. And beloved Father, all that I can return for these many gifts is a love so great that it threatens to tear me in two. I love Thee from the inner most corners of my soul. I beg for the priceless favor of being allowed to serve Thee. All that my heart is crying and that my words cannot express, I know Thou, Heavenly Father, understandeth. I can say no more."
—Compilation, "Star of the West," Volume 10, Abbas Effendi

INTRODUCTION

by Eva Herr

I AM JUST A WOMAN who, like many, had a mystical experience after the occurrence of a very dark night of the soul. The full story can be referenced in my first book, *Agape: The Intent of the Soul*. A severe "dark night" followed by sudden illumination also seems to be a theme shared by everyone I have interviewed.

In my case, the experience was completely unexpected and brought with it a sudden and powerful mystical experience that occurred literally overnight while I slept. It instantaneously and radically changed what I had always known my life to be into something totally different. Prior to this event, I was caught up in the dogma of materialism, vanity, and self-consumed ideations. When I awoke the next morning, I was a different person with a different agenda in life . . . to fully understand consciousness—the God force—behind everything that exists. Accompanying this was a powerful but simplistic idea of agape—the love for one's fellow man as one loves oneself, because we are all one. I no longer cared about materialism, vanity, and my "me-me" attitude. From that moment on, my focus was no longer what others could do for me, but what could I do for others. This was a new approach for me.

I awoke with knowledge of cutting-edge science and alternative medicine that I had not previously known, plus an ability to accurately detect illness in others, often years in the future. Where did this come from? What did it mean? Was my mind playing tricks, or was the knowledge I received real? Was it in any form provable from a scientific perspective, and if it was, what did it mean to me, the people I know, and to the world?

A sudden, unquenchable thirst for knowledge drove me to seek what I could find regarding such matters; so, with a background in litigation and research skills, I set out to find the most factually based information available, from some of the most respected scientists in the world today. I have set forth my discoveries in this book.

What was the purpose of this *mystical experience* I had? What caused it to happen? What did it do? Is there more than one kind? How is it that consciousness conveys information from Big Mind (Source, God, The Force . . . whatever you want to call it) to little mind—the "who we are every day."

This book emerged by way of much contemplation and many long hours of conversations between my dear friend, Roy Scruggs, Ph.D., and me over the course of many years, focusing on the topic of the science of consciousness. Roy was a very interesting man; very educated in the physical sciences, aero engineering, as well as the meta-sciences, such as quantum mechanics and metaphysics. He was a very spiritual, astro-engineer who worked on the Apollo Project. Bottom line: he knew science and spiritual mysticism inside out.

I searched the globe over for the most brilliant and knowledgeable minds existing in the world today. The pre-requisite was that whatever they presented in our interview had to be of a sound scientific basis. This is where Roy came in. He and I sat for hundreds of hours, going over the materials presented by each scientist, whom I would then question on their views during my weekly radio show *Infinite Consciousness*. I asked the hard questions. I didn't want to know what they *thought* I wanted to know that they *knew*. What were their positions on certain topics, and why did they stand so firmly on these positions? What research was available to prove what they had come to believe?

One thing I learned from my experience is that we are one with everything . . . that there is in fact no matter on the quantum level . . . meaning, that we are not separate from anything else in existence. I began to wonder if science had proven this, or if science even thought they were on the horizon of proving it. How could it be that there is no separation between us and everything else? It all boils down to the fact that matter does not exist on the quantum level. So my search began for the facts.

It has been my honor to have had the opportunity to study and learn with some of the most brilliant minds of our times. Over the past decade I have studied, meditated, and prepared for these questions of such great importance, and conducted numerous interviews with these remarkable scientists through my radio show. I think you will find the result to be some of the most astonishing and thought-provoking material you will ever read and I hope that it will give you hope for your life and the future of our children, our planet and the generations to come.

AND THIS IS HOW IT ALL STARTED . . . .

Notes for the Scientists by Roy Scruggs, Ph.D. and Eva Herr

WE ARE CONCERNED WITH THE question: does the presence of sensate awareness or cognitive awareness or both assure that consciousness is active? Are these attributes of consciousness? Are they signifiers of consciousness? Can consciousness be active without the presence of either one of these attributes/signifiers? In this latter case would it be correct to say that consciousness exists merely "in potential"? Would it then follow that consciousness could be seen as something like a field (as the term is used scientifically)?

A few concerns as an opening gambit:

1. Cognitive dualities and the cognitive universe

   a) Can we construct a coherent hierarchy of duals?

2. Awareness: sensate, cognitive, and self

3. Awareness and physical embodiment

4. Awareness and mind

   a) Cognitive awareness implies thinking and infers brain processing

b) Does the mind think or does it simply know?

5. Will as action, intention as potential

6. Can states be expressions of consciousness?

7. States as consequence of intention

8. Physical evidence: extra-normal phenomena

   a) Is intention mediated by consciousness?

   b) In some e-normal experiments consciousness looks like a "field" mediating intention

9. The inter-play of intention, awareness, and consciousness in realization

The model below is an attempt at a concise statement of the view expressed in Buddhist thought to the effect that the entire universe is rationally constructed of duals, or "Yin-Yang" pairings, each engaged in an unending dance of near-equilibrium opposition. The collapse of the universe of duals is tantamount to reduction to, or return to, the One. One could say that when the dance is over the One remains. Note the distinction between the above scheme and the usual assertion made about self-awareness: if I am A, and assert that "I am not B," then it follows that "I am not B" applies to every other thing in the universe. In the above construction the negation applies only to the dual of A.

Reflecting on the partial list of issues listed above, it becomes evident that the scope of inquiry about the nature of consciousness can quickly become unmanageable. This suggests that any further inquiry in this area, which has gone on without conclusion for millennia, needs to be conducted piecemeal. If each piece can be developed in a self-consistent manner and then the pieces integrated in a mutually consistent manner, the result, somewhere down the road, could be of great benefit.

These writers would propose that a good place to start with our clean sheet of paper is in regard to clear and quantitative issues concerning the widespread phenomena variously called paranormal or extra-normal events. We have also found through discussions that the word "consciousness" has many different meanings to different people and that it is imperative that we define what it is we are talking about when attempting to communicate on this topic. We have found that when conversing on this topic there is generally no meeting of the minds as to exactly what we are trying to convey, and that there is not even an awareness that there is no meeting of the minds. For example "consciousness" has been defined as "awareness," "zero point field," "ground of all being," "irreducible unit," God, etc. This is a significant problem with linguistics. How can the science community ever communicate effectively, if there is no meeting of the minds about that which is being discussed? What is exactly is meant by the word "consciousness"?

We have much experimental evidence, carefully quantified in terms of physical correlates, that something beyond our present comprehension is at work in these phenomena. Because there are in fact clear, indisputable, and abiding physical consequences of the many experiments (and indeed fairly common experiences for some individuals), there is room for theory building to take place. The fact is that science today has not the slightest notion what mediates the results recorded in these events.

Is it really enough to say that "consciousness collapses the state-vector" in quantum mechanical processes? If instead we say "consciousness mediates the formation of the measured state-vector" then we are compelled in all scientific honesty to pursue an understanding of what consciousness is, at least in the context of the current question. These writers hasten to add the considered opinion that quantum theory is not a good example because it is a flawed physical theory, although a very good engineering theory. Never has the observation that "the map is not the territory" so clearly applied as in quantum theory (as distinct from quantum mechanics, which is clearly defined phenomenally). The phenomenal results for paranormal experiments are at least as well defined as the phenomenal results obtained in quantum mechanical experiments. The real question is in what way do these different processes depend on consciousness? Are the same attributes of consciousness at work in each such instance? For example, the measured result of non-locality in quantum mechanics appears to be very similar in nature to the measured results in paranormal experiments exhibiting remote influence.

While quantum theory cannot exclude non-locality, it also cannot explain it. This says in neither of the two cases, quantum or paranormal, do we have a theoretical model describing how local and non-local events become correlated, apparently without respect for distance or even time. These writers maintain that quantum entanglement has about as much explanatory power as, say, "epiphenomenon." It is maintained by Dr. Scruggs that the case for conscious influence is relatively weak in quantum theoretical exposition, but relatively strong by the direct evidence available in paranormal investigations.

Here are some thoughts on defining "self."

We have noted that there are three well-recognized aspects of awareness:

1. *Sensate Awareness.* This aspect is widespread in the natural world. Even plants have been shown to have this property. The presence of sensate awareness can be demonstrated by clearly defined experimental methods.

2. *Cognitive Awareness.* This aspect is not so widespread. It is known by experiment to be present in some mammals, particularly humans. Again, the demonstration of this is unambiguous.

3. *Self-Awareness.* This aspect is widely recognized as existing, but is generally thought to be subjective. A certain kind of internal awareness that is distinct from the senses and cognition. There is no known physical experiment that can quantify this aspect, so some researchers, particularly in AI, tend to think of this as epiphenomenal.

At this time these writers consider awareness and consciousness to be distinct but definitely not independent. Thus anything we say about awareness in general and self- awareness in particular has a bearing on our consideration of issues of consciousness.

It is proposed to develop an initially qualitative model of ego or self (as distinct from Self, which is considered a transcendent expression of being) which will have appeal for scientific thinkers inquiring about the nature of consciousness and its effects in physical phenomena. We believe that a well-ordered modeling of self will be of value in our search for meaning in the elusive phenomenon called consciousness. To this end we refer again to the sketch presented earlier in this memo regarding the construction of duals. We would like to explore a conception of self as constituted of a perhaps vast collection of duals of the type mentioned above. One must take care that such a model be composed of duals that are non-intersecting. By that is meant that no dual infers any other dual. For example if we have a dual (light/dark) and a dual (hot/cold), nothing about one infers anything about the other. A "state of self" exists when the entire set of duals takes on a definite state. This state concept is of course highly dynamic, changing constantly. But changing in some irreducible set of duals does not imply that self is necessarily an epiphenomenon. By way of metaphor, we could relate this conception of self to the existence in quantum mechanics of macroscopic structures called "condensates." These are coherent particulate structures that represent an extremum energy state for a given quantized material system. One such condensate is that identified with Bose and Einstein. There are other such examples. The difference between the two conceptions in one particular aspect is that a condensate is stable, whereas self may or may not be. One could envision a stable state of self-existing, for example, when one is engaged in meditation. Here the self would be more or less suspended in time and exist in an extremum (minimum) state.

If a self is characterized in general by an n-space of duals one must ask what is meant by a "minimum" state of self. This suggests that the number of active duals, as well as the individual states of the duals, has a part to play in each instantiation of self.

It is suggested by the meditative experiences of eastern as well as western mystics that a state of "no-self" is attainable. Such a result would be consistent in the dual model outlined above with collapsing all the duals to the "I-am" case.

The possibility of correlating a self-state with an external physical state comes immediately to mind. Let us say that a particular self-state is thought to support a particular intention. This intention might be to alter the behavior of a random event generator (REG). It is then reasonable to ask whether the state of the REG might be correlated with the self-state. This line of inquiry is in some way perhaps related to the well-known non-locality effects in quantum mechanics, which are shown to exhibit state correlations for remote events.

There are two approaches available for beginning to develop a model for the something that we generally refer to as consciousness. We believe that the above discussion of the various levels of awareness must constitute at least a part of such an overarching model. It is the position of the writers, at least at the present time, that the word "consciousness" ought to be tentatively reserved to characterize something that is field-like and which is the prime mediator of the projection of intention. The strength of the projected intention can be thought of as somehow proportional to the level of attention brought to bear. Here we mean by attention simply the level or quality of one or more of the levels of awareness discussed above. The first possible approach to this task is a reductionist view of modeling, wherein principles are recognized and a model is developed based on a logical application of any available principles. The second approach is a holistic one, in which models for various phenomena are empirically developed and their commonality in the end is what establishes the emergent principles. In other words, one approach is bottom-up while the other is top-down.

CHAPTER 1

Robert Jahn, Ph. D. and Brenda Dunn

Robert Jahn was Dean Emeritus of the School of Engineering and Applied Science. He is a Fellow of the American Physical Society and of the American Institute of Aeronautics and Astronautics, and has been chairman of the AIAA Electric Propulsion Technical Committee, associate editor of the AIAA Journal, and a member of the NASA Space Science and Technology Advisory Committee. He is vice president of the Society for Scientific Exploration and chairman of the board of the International Consciousness Research Laboratories consortium.

Brenda Dunne is president and treasurer of International Consciousness Research Laboratories and was laboratory manager of the Princeton Engineering Anomalies Research (PEAR) Laboratory. She holds a Masters degree in developmental psychology from the University of Chicago and also serves as education officer of the Society for Scientific Exploration.

Eva: Brenda, please tell us a little bit about what PEAR Lab is and what you did there.

Brenda: I was the Laboratory Manager of PEAR, which stands for Princeton Engineering Anomalies Research. It was a program that looked at the role of consciousness in physical reality, and had been housed here in the Mechanical and Aerospace Engineering Department of Princeton University since 1979. The program was established by Professor Robert Jahn, who was its director.

An amazing man himself.

Yes, indeed . . . and very definitely my hero. Bob Jahn was dean of the School of Engineering and Applied Science when he set this program in motion. He is an aerospace engineer whose main area of research for some forty-odd years has been in advanced aerospace propulsion systems, very basic hard-core rocket science. He served as dean of the school for fifteen years, and when his third term was up he returned to teach in his home department, which is why the program is situated there.

PEAR has three major portions to it. The largest component evolved from the original student project, and is a body of experiments wherein human operators attempt to influence or interact with various types of random physical processes or systems with an intention to influence their statistical output distributions in accordance with their pre-stated and prerecorded intentions.

In laymen's terms, what does that mean?

We are asking in these experiments whether human intention can actually affect the physical behavior of various kinds of engineering devices. By pure intentionality I mean there are no physical connections, no sensory contact between the human operator and the machines. The question is whether our consciousness can interact with these devices to make a difference in a physical process that can be measured and evaluated by standard scientific terms.

What is your overall success rate in proving that it does?

Well, if you look across all the experiments we've done in the last twenty-seven years, and do a kind of meta-analysis, we're talking about the likelihood of these effects being due to chance as a few parts per billion. What does that mean in laymen's terms? It means that effects are very probably real.

Let me back up to describe the other two parts of the program, as they all come together. The other part of our research program involves a phenomenon called remote perception, where people attempt to obtain information about remote locations, with no sensory input. Here, our efforts have been to attempt to measure how much information is actually being acquired in this process. As with our human/machine experiments, once again we have found that a very significant component of extra-chance information is being acquired by people who are just trying to envision where another person is at an assigned time.

What is particularly striking about the results of both of these experiments is that the anomalous effects seem to be totally independent of how far away the person is, spatially, and even more surprisingly, how far away they are temporally. In other words, people are able to influence events and describe scenes that can be thousands of miles away, up to several days before or after the location has been identified. So what we are learning from this is that these anomalous effects, this ability of consciousness to generate information that can affect the physical world, or acquire information from the physical world by non-sensory means, is real, and can be demonstrated under controlled, scientific conditions. The implication is that consciousness is non-local, independent of distance and time, and therefore not dependent in any evident causal manner on the physical brain.

The third part of our program consists of attempts to explain these extraordinary events within a scientific framework. The implications, of course, are that the current models that we have of the way the world works are far from complete. It's not that they're wrong, but they're limited . . . and these data, these studies are showing us that they won't be complete until we can come up with models of reality that can take into account our consciousness, and the subjective qualities that are associated with consciousness. This is something that the world of hard science has not been comfortable in acknowledging up until now. We cannot have a complete picture of the world until we acknowledge that we are part of that world; we are not just passive observers.

The mental world and the physical world are not two separate things, as Descartes proposed several hundred years ago. They are intertwined in a way. They're complementary; they are two different ways of looking at reality, and they are each legitimate. Science acknowledges that the physical representations are legitimate, but they are very uncomfortable with the mental ones. They are harder to measure, for one thing.

But if it is so obvious that it is real, how can it be denied?

It's very hard for people in the world of science to concede that maybe they're wrong. In a sense, these findings challenge the authority of science. But they also raise some questions that we can't answer yet. How does it work? How could this be? What are the parameters that bear on these phenomena? You know, when you start to say things like space or time might actually be subjective rather than objective components of the physical world . . . that can be scary.

What do you mean by objective and subjective?

Our current scientific worldview assumes that space and time are qualities of the physical world. What our results are suggesting is that they are qualities of the mind. They may not necessarily be components. I shouldn't say *necessarily*; they are not *solely* components of the outside world. They seem to be ways of measuring the interaction between the mind and the physical world; the inside and the outside. Now, while this evidence is troublesome from the point of view of hard-core quantitative science, it has some wonderful implications on a very pragmatic and personal level.

Does that mean, if true, that if the entire world focused on treating one another like they themselves want to be treated, the world would have instant peace?

I don't know about *instant*, but it would certainly be a lot more peaceful. Isn't this the message from just about all of the great world religions? Love your neighbor as yourself?

Yes, it is. And PEAR has proven that emotions manifest health.

Absolutely.

Do you believe that it happens through frequencies or vibrations?
I think disease comes in from the spiritual level, not the other way around.

I need to point out that when one speaks of frequencies, it's probably a good idea to distinguish how one is using the term, because the folks that deal in the physical representations of frequencies and amplitudes tend to get a little uncomfortable when you start dragging their language into the world of spiritual implications. We see this all the time. When we attempt to develop theoretical models that might accommodate the anomalies in a viable conceptual framework, one of the things that has proven useful is to think in terms of information, rather than energy. Of course, frequencies are a form of information. So, I don't think we are on a totally different wavelength, so to speak.

Do you think information is encoded within frequencies?

Again, I can't speak in the language of frequencies. I'm not a physicist. But also, because the term has such broad meaning . . . .

How about electromagnetism?

I think electromagnetism, like time and space, is simply an ordering principle of consciousness. All of these laws and rules are actually constructs of consciousness that have proven useful for ordering and organizing its experience of the world around it. I don't think one can speak of them as being solely the product of the physical world, or solely as product of the mind.

This is obviously something that will create conflict with some people. We were talking about the definition of consciousness. What would be a good definitive word or description for that?

We tend to prefer the word "information," simply because information implies some sort of ordered pattern, as opposed to chaos. So we are talking order and chaos in a way. As such, one can then say that what consciousness does, or is, is an ordering principle. This works rather well whether you are spelling consciousness with small "c" or a capital "C." "Frequency" has an implication that tends to be related more specifically to physical transmissions. The same with "electromagnetism." These concepts are based on certain rules that define their applications, and our anomalous phenomena do not conform to those rules. Electromagnetic fields, for example, tend to get weaker with increased distance; the further away you get, the weaker the signal gets. This is not the case with our experimental data.

Like the light of a light bulb. The further away you get, the less you see.

Exactly. Now, our experimental effects don't seem to get weaker the further away one gets, whether in space or in time. But information is a concept that is non-local, and is dependent on a specific frame of reference, which is essentially a subjective variable.

Would you agree that we have three levels of awareness: sensate, cognitive, and self?

This is a question of language, and one's frame of reference. It depends on what you mean by these terms.

I'm trying to define awareness, or consciousness, for people who might have no idea what we are talking about.

I would say that there are three levels, but those would not be the words I would use. I think I would talk about physical, mental, and spiritual . . . if that's the same thing that you mean.

Yes, I think it is.

You know, we can argue about the words, of course; that's what leads to highly organized religions or scientific domains of study. In these cases, rather than trying to find the common features, people tend to fight over the proper words.

Let's look at brain vs. mind. Mind, to me, is contained within consciousness, but I separate it from the physical brain, in what they do. Would you say that the brain thinks? Does it process, or does it create thinking?

I think the brain is, in a sense, the transducer, if you will, of consciousness, which allows the processes of consciousness to manifest or to be expressed and communicated in the physical world. Much the way television or radio somehow transforms the waves, the programming, into something that you can tune into and pick up and see or hear.

Much like a computer?

In a way yes. In a television or a radio, the waves are out there. If I'm in a room and I don't have a radio or I have one and it's not on, the program or the information in those programs is there potentially. It doesn't mean it doesn't exist until I turn my radio on. But I can't access it without the radio. I think our brains probably work something like that. I don't think consciousness, as Bob Jahn and I would use the term, since I speak for both of us, is physical in nature.

When a lot of people speak of consciousness, they are speaking of the cognitive activity of our physical brains—attention, language, cognition . . . whatever. When we use the term, we are speaking in a much more general sense. We're speaking of the world of subjective experience.

Of awareness?

Not even awareness. One can be sleeping and not be consciously aware, but consciousness is still present, just not following the usual rules of language or everyday cognition. Think of it this way. Think of the so-called distinction, if there is one, between "I" and "not I." The "not I" is what we experience as the "out there," the world. Then there is the subjective. Anything that I would regard as me, anything that comes into the category of me-ness, that subjective aspect, I would call consciousness. Anything that is outside that I would regard as not me, I call environment. But of course that interaction, even that distinction, is a very subjective one. I might sometimes refer to my body almost as if it were independent of me. But other times I accept that my body and I are the same thing. So that distinction now becomes very situation-specific. I think it is because it is really one anyway and it's just a question of where you want to draw the line of distinction.

When we fall in love, that distinction between "I" and "not I" gets pretty blurry and we become a "we." Now the "you" versus "me" is no longer as relevant. You have traded them in for a "we." This can go on into much vaster dimensions as well. And it may be in that domain that the effect of the mind on physical health comes into play. If we think our of bodies as somehow objective physical things, then of course, we don't think in terms of being like part of the "I," it's part of the "it." But when we recognize that the "I" and "not I" are sort of merging and that where I draw that line is a matter of choice, then, hey, there's no longer a distinction between "I," my spirit, if you will, "I" my mind, and "I" my body. If my mind can be shown to affect the way some physical process such as a machine sitting on the table in front of me, then it's not too big a jump to say why can't my mind affect the way the processes that are going on in my body are behaving?

Has anyone been able to turn a light on or off from a distance?

Not under controlled conditions, to the best of my knowledge. That's not something we've tested. It is, however, a phenomenon that is frequently reported. It's funny I think not a week goes by that we don't get three or four letters from people who have had experiences of lights turning off or something like that. They can't wear watches without them breaking, and so forth.

They can't control that though, right?

It doesn't appear to be something they control consciously, but it seems to happen pretty frequently, because we've gotten literally hundreds of such reports. We can't do anything with these reports, and if I may ask readers, please don't write to us with your experiences, because we really can't study them or help you with them or give you any advice on how to control it. All we can do is tell you "yes, we hear this a lot."

What we want to do here in our laboratory is study stuff that we can control under laboratory conditions, and these tend to be very tiny effects that are statistical in nature. But they can add up over many tens or hundreds of thousands of such events to highly unlikely alterations of what would be expected. So yes, people do seem capable of turning off light bulbs. You hear of so-called poltergeist phenomena . . . large scale, macroscopic anomalies. I am quite persuaded these are real events, and I think if we can get to a point where we can understand the little stuff, maybe we would be in a position to extrapolate to how this might affect the more significant large-scale stuff. All we can say now is that the structure of information is being altered, and of course information is what consciousness deals in.

What do you think those anomalies are? Souls? Some kind of energy?

Boy that is not an easy question. I'm going to speak now on the basis of my own intuition, rather than that of empirical evidence. From what I've seen and what little I do understand, these events seem to arise from some kind of uncertainty. What do I mean by uncertainty . . . when something is neither "a" nor "b." Physicists sometimes speak of the Schrödinger's cat paradox, where a cat is in a box and there is a pellet of poison there that has a 50 percent likelihood of being activated, but you can't tell until you look whether the cat is alive or dead. So until you look, the cat is in a state that is potentially both alive and dead. In our interactions with the physical world, there is this domain of uncertainty that is neither "a" nor "b."

To get back to something that most of us can relate to, let's talk about love again. When you fall in love, or when you are in love, you have an "I" and a "you" and a "we." When you speak of the "we," it is neither "I" nor "you." When the "I" and the "you" merge, the distinction between them becomes very vague. The "we" doesn't really have a sharp distinction between "you" and "me." In that domain of overlap between two potential realities, the reality of "you" and the reality of "me" can no longer be sharply differentiated. You have a certain gray area of uncertainty. I think that's where these things come from.

Have you witnessed any anomalies involving emotions?

I think they have to do with emotion, with need, with resonance (which is another way to say love), with intention, desire, meaning . . . all of these things are of course not physical variables. They're subjective variables, but they are the ones that again and again seem to be the relevant factors in our studies. This is what people talk about when they get effects. They say, "I feel like I've become one with the machine." It's like playing a musical instrument or driving a car. They can no longer distinguish sharply between the self and the machine, and that act of differentiating is the way consciousness organizes experience. It imposes information—this, not that; you, not me; in, not out; mind, not matter. But in that domain where you can't any longer make that distinction, is it mind or matter? Is it you or me? Yes. Is it in or out? Yes, and no . . . because those distinctions are no longer sharp, no longer viable forms of information. It is that blurry area that is what I'm referring to when I say *uncertainty*. That's where I think these phenomena arise from. They are anomalous because they don't fit either world. They are somehow the product of the interaction of two aspects of reality coming together; an overlap, if you will. I hope this makes sense to your readers because I don't know how else to say it.

It might take a bit of focus and thought to follow some of what you say, but you are making a lot of sense.

Well, in our minds we are trained to make these distinctions. From the time we are little kids, this is blue, this is yellow, this is green, you know. This is up, this is down, but those distinctions are creations of the mind. Up and down are relative to the way our minds perceive and represent.

This raises something someone told me the other day about people who see things upside down. Something happens to them—they get hit on the head or something—and then train their mind so that after a while, the perceptual reversal seems normal.

Yes. Again, there's the brain doing its thing, processing and categorizing information. It takes the potential information from the environment—whether it's through the eyes or ears or touch or whatever—and transforms it into vibrations, if you will; electromagnetic signals, and the brain can then process it to represent images or sounds or feelings or tastes or what not. But some of this may be learned; it's not just hard-wired.

Different cultures have different ways of creating or representing experience. In our culture, for example, we have many different models of cars. If I'm into cars, I could probably rattle off twenty different models and makes of cars. But then there's the famous example of Eskimos having twenty different words for snow. We don't, since snow is not as essential to our livelihood and lifestyles as cars are. But, snow is essential to the Eskimos' reality. It is such a central component of their culture and their world that they have to have a much more finely differentiated way of representing it. On the other hand, they probably couldn't care less between one model of automobile or one brand of toothpaste or another. So again, our society, our culture, and our education are all telling us where we should discriminate and what things should be important. If I am a botanist by profession, I'm going to know a lot of different names for a lot of different kind of trees. If you are a musician, you are going to have a lot of information about different types of sounds or musical notations and maybe a tree is a tree is a tree to you. But are there separate worlds where there are trees and where there is music? It is one world. It is our minds, our desires, and our intentions that say I am going to focus on the world of trees, or of music. You may decide to focus on the world of music, while an Eskimo focuses on the world of snow. So we are creating realities in which each of us is going to get more and more complex and subtle nuances of distinction in our personal worlds. Taken far enough, we can no longer communicate with each other.

They say a specialist is someone who knows more and more about less and less until they know everything about nothing. Then there's the generalist, who knows less and less about more and more and eventually knows nothing about everything! Those two categories probably give you a fairly good summary of what I think consciousness is. Consciousness does both of these. It discriminates and it generalizes. Those are probably its two main tools. It does this on a conscious level when we are awake. But it also does it on an unconscious level—our body functions, our dreams, our instinctive reactions to things, and what not. We are processing information all of the time, but not all of it is cognitive. Some of it is the information that is conveyed by the stuff that is in the air we breathe or the water we drink. I may not cognitively or consciously be aware of that, but my body knows it.

Let's turn to how thought manifests into physical reality, or emotions manifest illness in the body, and maybe why what goes around comes around. We wouldn't stand in a metal fishing boat in a lightning storm, because water conducts electricity. I believe that when you think a thought, that's exactly what happens: a tiny electrical lightning bolt occurs. Since there is no separation between mind and matter, I wonder if it could be the firing of an electron, or smaller unit thereof, for negative thought, because that would be negativity energy. The negative energy would not realize it was contained within a skull; it goes out into the world and brings back negative things. We know atoms transmit and receive at the same time wouldn't that be a good reason why what goes around, comes around?

It's as good a model as any. Of course, we need to remember that any model that we create of the way the world works is a reflection of our minds as well what we are describing.

I'd just love people to have a scientific reason for such things.

I would not necessarily agree with what you are saying. Not that I disagree with the principle of what you are saying, but the language, once again, is based on and presumes a fairly physical, reductionist paradigm. It assumes that all experience, including our thoughts, can be explained by physically based concepts like atoms or electrons or what not. I would take a more complementary view that says the atoms and electrons are themselves constructions of consciousness. So, the fundamental stuff of the universe is not the physical atoms and electrons, but our ideas or experiences of these. Atoms and electrons are simply terms or concepts that we employ to describe these experiences or ideas, not the experiences or ideas as such. Consciousness is that which has an experience and attempts to describe that experience, and invokes metaphors such as electrons and atoms to do so. Reality is the interaction of consciousness with what it experiences, subjectively, and represents, objectively.

Let me try to present a very simple and short representation of one of our own models and the way that we have tried to approach your question about how thought might manifest into physical reality. Visualize a square. Now divide that square into quarters; you now have a square with four little squares inside. Now, on the left-hand side, you have two squares, and on the right-hand side, you have two squares. Let's label the left-hand side "mind" and label the right-hand side "matter."

Now let's look at the top two squares and the bottom two squares. The top two squares, whether mind or matter, we will call "conscious" or "tangible." On the upper left is the world of the conscious mind, the brain activity, in the "not being in a coma" definition, and on the upper right is the world, the domain of the tangible physical world—the tables, chairs, atoms, electrons, and so forth. Now, when you go to the bottom layer, you're dealing with the world of the intangible. On the left side, underneath the domain of the conscious mind, as you go deeper and deeper, you find yourself in the domain of the unconscious or subconscious. We're not always aware of these. When we wake up out of a dream, for example, that dividing line can sort of slosh back and forth. Sometimes we have little glimpses from the conscious mind into the unconscious. But that unconscious goes pretty deep until you get down to the world of what Jung called the archetypes, or universal symbols. It's no longer thoughts or specific brain experiences, it is something much more abstract.

Same thing goes on now on the left-hand side underlying the world of physical expression. You have the subatomic world of quantum mechanics, of string theory, or quarks, or the potentialities of the zero point field. These things are no longer dealing with tangible stuff; they all come down to being represented in terms of possibilities. The same thing goes on in the consciousness side of the house. The deeper you go, the thinner and thinner the distinction between the two sides becomes. At some deep fundamental level, the world of the deep unconscious and the world of deep physical potential is the same stuff. It's just all sloshing back and forth. It's some primordial Source, if you will, with a capital "S."

Now, maybe what is going on is that the conscious mind has an intention. "I want to get more highs than lows," in an experiment. "I have a desire to get in touch with someone I haven't spoken to in a while," or something on that order. If that desire, that intention, is deep enough, and meaningful enough, to get below the superficial level and down into the world of the unconscious, it can possibly actually affect the potentiality—the probability of what is going to manifest in the physical world—and make it a little bit more likely that you'll get a call from that person, or that you'll get more heads than tails in the experiment.

It may go the other way around. Somebody is thinking of you and maybe, if you can stop thinking cognitively long enough—suspended in those daydream states we get into, or just sort of staring into space and not thinking of anything in particular—maybe then we become more receptive and then all of a sudden, out of nowhere, I think of Eva. "Gee, I wonder how Eva is doing? I haven't talked to her in ages. Maybe I'll give her a call." Now who is influencing whom? Can you even speak of causality? Or are you simply speaking of a connectedness there that, when we are open to it, affects both the domain of the mental and the domain of the physical simultaneously, because ultimately they are coming from the same source.

There is no separation.

The separation itself does not even exist at the most fundamental level. That's where I think the action is. That, of course, is the domain of uncertainty that the founders of quantum mechanics talked about, because you can't say whether an experience is physical or mental. It's both and neither.

I hope this has been helpful, and I'd like to take the opportunity to say that what you are doing is just great. So many people out there are really hungry to understand these topics and they're not always getting very straight answers. They frequently get very biased views one way or another, and when people like you come along trying to provide an open-minded and broadly representative span of perspectives on these tough topics, it is such a great benefit. I know from my own mail, and my own phone calls, there is a need for this. So thank you for putting this out there, and thank you for giving me the opportunity to contribute to it.

CHAPTER 2

Christian de Quincey, Ph.D.

Christian de Quincey is professor of philosophy and consciousness studies at John F. Kennedy University, dean of consciousness studies at the University of Philosophical Research, and adjunct faculty at the Holmes Institute. He is founder of The Wisdom Academy and author of the award-winning book *Radical Nature: The Soul of Matter* as well as *Radical Knowing: Understanding Consciousness through Relationship.* His latest books are *Consciousness from Zombies to Angels* and *Deep Spirit: Cracking the Noetic Code.*

Eva: Please tell us a little about your background.

Christian: I have a Ph.D. in philosophy and religion, and a master's degree in consciousness studies. I teach philosophy and consciousness studies at John F. Kennedy University in northern California and at the University of Philosophical Research in Burbank, southern California. I am also the founder of the Wisdom Academy, an online service that offers mentorships in consciousness and conscious transformation.

I have been interested in consciousness studies pretty much as far back as I can remember. Since I was a kid of seven or eight, I have been fascinated with the question, "What is the relationship between the mind and the body, and how can we explain it?" That question has really become the focus of my career: "What is the nature of, and relationship between, consciousness and energy, between mind and matter, between mind and body, and how can our understanding of that relationship be empowering to our lives?" Although I am trained in philosophy, I am not interested just in logical, rational explanations of things. I am interested in how understanding consciousness can lead to transformation in our lives. The philosophy I teach includes other ways of knowing, such as feeling and intuition, as well as our senses and rationality.

Your book, Consciousness from Zombies to Angels, *is excellent. I would love to have a second conversation on just that book.*

Thank you. I've written a couple of other books as well. On my personal website, www.ChristiandeQuincey.com, readers can find out more about my other books, including *Radical Knowing*, which is about understanding consciousness through relationship. My fourth book, *Deep Spirit: Cracking the Noetic Code*, is a novel about the evolution of consciousness from light to enlightenment.

What is your definition of consciousness? I like to start here so everyone will know what we are talking about.

Ah, yes. I teach a lot of courses on consciousness, as well as having written a lot on the topic, and the one thing I always avoid doing is defining consciousness. I have a couple of reasons for this. First, to define something is by definition to limit it, to put boundaries around it, and I think it is premature to decide in advance what the limits of consciousness might be, or indeed if there are any limits. That's one meaning of "definition," but there's another meaning. A definition usually refers to an objective, standard meaning. We go to a dictionary to find an objective meaning of a word, and the one thing we know about consciousness is that it is not objective—it is *subjective*.

So, I don't see how anyone can claim to have *the* correct definition or *the* correct meaning of consciousness. However, I think it is important for us to clarify what we *mean* when we use the word "consciousness." So that is what I do. In my books, lectures, and classes, I take time to clarify what I mean by consciousness.

To simplify: Consciousness is the ability to *know*, be *aware*, and to make *choices*. That's the essence of consciousness: to be aware, to have an ability to know something, and to make choices. Anything that can be aware of anything else, including itself, and that can make choices necessarily has consciousness. That's the simplest meaning.

You said the "essence" of consciousness. Does that mean those are attributes of consciousness?

Well, yes, you could say they are attributes . . . they are also the essence in the sense that they are intrinsic to the nature of consciousness. Consciousness is what it is to be aware of anything, to know anything, to feel anything, and to be able to make choices. So consciousness is able to feel and sense possibilities in every moment. Then it can make choices between those possibilities, about how we act.

Would it be fair to say that consciousness—again, language may be a problem here—is the ground of all being?

I don't go quite that far; I would say that consciousness is *intrinsic* to the ground of all being. In other words, there is no part of being that doesn't have some kind of consciousness going on. But consciousness is not the whole story. Consciousness, as I said, is the ability to be aware, to create intentions, and to make choices. Something else is needed besides the ability to create intentions and make choices; we also need to be able to *act*—to take action— and that's where energy comes in. So the world, the ground of being, is composed of both consciousness and energy. They are not the same; they are distinct.

Nevertheless, in my work, I propose that consciousness and energy always go together. You can never have one without the other. So a world that consisted of only pure consciousness would be a world where nothing ever happens, or *could* ever happen. There could only be passive observation. Without energy, nothing ever happens. With pure consciousness, all the greatest intentions in the world could be made but they could never be manifested;

they could never be acted on unless there was also energy to make things happen. Therefore, since quite obviously events *do happen* and are *experienced,* the ground of being must be both consciousness *and* energy. I'm not saying that energy and consciousness are identical; they are distinct, but they always go together.

What do you believe to be the source of the original intention? How do you think that came to be?

Let's see if this answers your question: There never was a beginning; the Source is eternal. It never had a beginning. It always existed, always had consciousness, and always had energy. There never was a time when there was pure *nothing.* Something always existed, and what existed consisted of *sentient energy:* energy that tingles with the spark of spirit.

Can you define mind for us? Or distinguish between Big Mind and little mind?

I use the terms "mind," "consciousness," and "experience" pretty much synonymously. Only when we need to identify different forms of consciousness do I find it useful to make a distinction between mind and consciousness. Here's how I view it. Reality consists of two main divisions, or "buckets" of being. One bucket we can label "nonphysical," and that consists of mind, experience, consciousness, soul, and spirit. The other bucket contains anything "physical," such as tables and chairs and cars and houses and clothes and everything made of matter. One bucket could be labeled "mind" and the other could be labeled "matter." We could call those two buckets "consciousness" and "energy." In short, reality consists of two domains: one is non-physical—the domain of mind, soul, spirit, consciousness; and the other is physical—the domain of matter, energy, and objects in space.

What about the phrases "Big Mind" and "little mind"?

Yes. "Big Mind" is what I would call in other contexts "cosmic consciousness." It is the consciousness of the entire cosmos. Other people might refer to it as God, or the Divine, or Spirit.

That is what I would consider "Big Mind." Little mind is our own egoic mind. To a large extent, that's the mind talking to you at the moment; and I assume you are communicating with me from your egoic mind, at least to some extent. Our egoic minds are always informed—if we are open to being informed—by the wisdom of the bigger mind. We get ourselves into difficulty and create personal, interpersonal, and social problems when we operate from the illusion that all that really exists is little mind. We don't open up to the greater wisdom of Mind in the Cosmos, the mind that exists in the world around us in nature and, throughout the universe.

Where do you think little mind resides?

Ah, now there is a great question. During the first week of a new course, I usually ask students: "Point to where you think your consciousness is." After a moment of hesitation, some will point to their heart and others to their head, while some will do what I call the "consciousness shuffle" —they kind of wave their arms about to indicate that consciousness is all over their bodies.

I then point out that it was a trick question. Mind or consciousness doesn't exist *anywhere*. Mind does not exist in space; it's not in your head, it's not in your brain, it's not in your heart, it's not in your stomach, it's not anywhere in your body. If you open up somebody's head or heart or stomach, you are never going see their mind or consciousness. Consciousness doesn't have that kind of existence. It doesn't exist in space the way objects exist in space. Consciousness is the *subject* that knows or feels or is aware of objects. It is not itself an object in space.

The real question to ask is not "*where* is consciousness" but "*when* is consciousness," and we all know the answer to that—it is right *now*. Consciousness is always *now, now, now, now, now*. It's important not to think of consciousness as an object that can exist in space the way tables and chairs and brains and computers do.

To what do you attribute the various gradients of consciousness in human beings, like the difference between someone who is "unconscious" and someone who is "awake"? If we were trying to explain the attributes of consciousness to someone whose consciousness is closed at a low level, perhaps locked down by fundamentalist beliefs . . . it would be like talking to a telephone pole, and we would appear to them as a "know-it-all." What do you attribute that to? Fields? Frequencies? Resonance? I'm not sure how to phrase this appropriately.

There are interesting and engaging issues bundled into that question. In my experience talking with Jehovah's Witnesses and other fundamentalists, it's not so much that they think *I'm* the know it all; I think they think I actually *don't* know it all because I don't share their beliefs. In fact, I think *they* are the "know-it-alls" because to them all the answers reside in their Bibles. Everything they need to know, everything anybody needs to know, is already printed in their gospels. This happens not to be a way I value for getting knowledge about what is real in the world.

To get back to your question, what accounts for a closed mind—whether it is the closed mind of a fundamentalist or the closed mind of a philosopher—I need to acknowledge that there are certainly times when my mind is closed and I am not aware that I am operating from my ego. Then I wake up and realize, "Oh, I've just been operating from my own ego," and do the best I can to open up and let go of that. So, what accounts for the lower levels of mind is the degree to which we are attached to our egos and identify with our egos.

This is not to say that the ego is wrong or a bad thing; it's not. Our egoic "I" evolved over millions of years to help us navigate our way through a very complex, and at times, dangerous world. So the ego has served us well. The problem is when the ego takes over—which it tries to do often—it wants us to identify our deepest self with *it*, and that's when things begin to spin out of control and create trouble. Only when we realize that we *have* an ego, not that we *are* an ego, do we begin to expand and open to different levels of consciousness. However, letting go of the ego is rarely, if ever, a one-time event. Eckhart Tolle may be an exception to that. He seems to have had an event in his life that was so transformative he liberated himself once and for all from the illusion that he is his ego.

It happened to me too.

Well, congratulations.

I don't know if it calls for congratulations . . .

Well, I think if you have liberated yourself permanently from the illusion that you are your ego that is a wonderful achievement. I think it would be a much better, safer, more harmonious world if more people achieve what you have achieved. I have a question: Why, when liberated, do we still continue to oscillate back and forth between enlightenment and illusion?

It certainly makes things more amenable to be here in everyday physical reality. What do you suppose causes one person to be so closed and another person to allow the awareness? Something happens there. Is it a frequency or a resonance? You know, the sound that comes from the universe is B flat. Is it something that has to do with a certain frequency that allows us to receive? Am I making any sense at all?

I understand what you are asking me, and I want to step back a little bit here and make a distinction. It's something I have noticed that is not familiar to a lot of people, particularly people who are interested in consciousness and the mind. Earlier in our conversation, I pointed out that the ground of being is not just consciousness, it is also energy, and I made a distinction between energy and consciousness. Here's the point: energy exists in space and consciousness does not exist in space, so anything that has resonance or vibrations and frequency exists in the domain of what I call the physical "bucket." Only things that extend in space can have vibrations. That is what vibration means: something moving or oscillating in space. Consciousness doesn't exist in space, so it doesn't actually have a vibration. It doesn't have a frequency.

How can some people pick it up and grab it even if they are not looking for it, and some people can't?

Because consciousness and energy always go together. When there is a shift in consciousness there is also a corresponding shift in the energy that goes with it. It's the *energy* that is vibrating, not the consciousness. So, if the energy of someone's body is vibrating, the consciousness associated with that body can feel the vibration—but the consciousness itself is not vibrating. It's the energy in the body. It could be the case that at a quantum level someone's body is in a much more coherent state and is vibrating that way. Then the consciousness associated with that body, with those vibrations, would itself be more coherent and harmonious, and therefore more open to communicating and picking up messages or meaning from other bodies around it—whether bodies of other human beings, other animals, or plants, the planet, or other galaxies . . . who knows what it might be. In any case, when consciousness is open, at a higher level of awareness, the body's energy will vibrate accordingly.

Let's go back to the example we gave earlier of the closed-minded fundamentalists. Being open or closed minded is deeply related to *beliefs* and *experience.* To be open, we need to cultivate what I call "*experience beyond belief.*" People often ask me what I believe about consciousness. I tell them that I do my best not to believe anything. And by the way, *I don't want you to believe anything I am saying.* I don't put a lot of trust or faith in belief. Why? Because a belief is made up of thoughts and thoughts are frozen fragments of consciousness. At every moment we are having an experience: *right now, right now, right now.* As soon as we have one moment of experience, it completes itself, is over, and it becomes something in the past. But it is immediately replaced by a new moment of experience—*right now, right now, right now.*

As we experience that process, we live in the present moment where consciousness exists. However, what tends to happen is, we then interpret that moment of experience by creating thoughts about it, and we accumulate all of these fragmented thoughts about experiences that once happened to us, whether it was just a moment ago, a month ago, a year ago, or a lifetime ago. We accumulate all of these frozen fragments of consciousness—our thoughts—and we hook them together into patterns that we think make sense, and then we form a belief about them. But because every belief is made of thoughts and every thought is a fragment of an expired experience, that means every belief is rooted in the past.

Meanwhile, experience is happening *right now* in the present moment. As long as we are attached to, focused on, and mesmerized by our beliefs, we are not paying attention as to what is actually happening *right now* in our experience, where wisdom lies. That's why I encourage people to be far less attached to what they believe. I have a practice or exercise for my students that encourages them to let go of their cherished beliefs—those beliefs they just absolutely know to be true. I invite them to let go of those beliefs, loosen up their attachment to them, and see what happens.

I guarantee that if you let go of your beliefs, you won't die. You won't evaporate. In fact, much more likely, you will experience a sense of liberation by paying attention to what you are actually *experiencing*. Experience is always open and creative—it is *actual*, present, brimming with possibilities. Experience, not belief, connects us to reality. Consciousness is happening *right now, right now, right now*, and that's exactly when reality happens: *right now, right now, right now*. The way to know reality is to experience reality through consciousness, not through our beliefs.

Does the presence of sensate and cognitive awareness, or both, ensure that consciousness is active? And do you believe these to be attributes of consciousness, or signifiers of consciousness?

Sensate and cognitive awareness? Yes I do. Any awareness already and automatically implies consciousness as I'm using the term. It would be impossible to have any kind of awareness, whether sensate or cognitive, unless some consciousness was present to do the "awaring." However, sensate and cognitive consciousness is not the whole story. We have other forms of consciousness, other ways of knowing, and we need to acknowledge, cultivate, and integrate them . . . such as feeling and intuition. These cannot be reduced to cognition or to information gathered through the senses.

Do you believe that consciousness can be active without the presence of either one of these attributes—sensation or cognition? If so, would it be correct to say that consciousness merely exists in potential?

Ah! That's probably one of the deepest questions we could get into: "Does consciousness just exist in potential?" I don't think it "just" exists in potential, because right now you and I are *actually* having a conversation. I am *actually* aware of listening to your questions. And because these are *actual* experiences and events, they're not just potential—they are actual. Consciousness is what brings possibility or potentiality into manifestation. We have learned this from quantum physics.

First of all, keep in mind that the entire physical world is built up from quantum events. A quantum system exists in a state of probabilities (or possibilities). Every quantum has a range of open options; it can manifest this way or that. However—and this is one of the strangest discoveries in modern science—every quantum system remains suspended in a state of probabilities *until an observation is made.* Only when a physicist (or any sentient being) observes a quantum system does it "collapse" from multiple probabilities to become an *actual* event. And since an observation is only an *observation* if someone *experiences* it that means *consciousness collapses the probabilities into actuality.* In other words, quantum reality shifts from possibility to manifestation only because consciousness is present.

Now that really is a startling scientific discovery. For the first time in more than four hundred years, science *has to* take consciousness into account in its quantum experiments otherwise the equations simply don't work out. It's momentous. To put it in plain language: *Consciousness creates physical reality.* Or, to be more accurate: consciousness *informs* physical reality. Consciousness shapes physical reality from the raw ingredients of quantum probabilities.

We could even express it in a bumper sticker that unites science and metaphysics:

Possibility + Consciousness = Manifestation

A quantum system remains in potential until it is observed, and the observer doesn't have to be a human scientist. It can be any sentient being. As soon as a quantum system is observed, what happens is called "the collapse of the quantum function," to use the technical language of physics. In other words, the possibilities collapse into one actuality and a quantum event occurs. Those events are the building blocks of the manifest real world we live in. If you like: consciousness is the connective tissue between the domain of possibilities and the domain of actuality . . . between what might be and what actually happens. Consciousness is the potency that brings possibility into manifestation.

Is it enough to say that consciousness collapses the state vector in quantum mechanical processes or should we say, "consciousness mediates the formation of the measured state vector?"

Well if consciousness *mediates*, I would need to know what it was mediating between. As far as I understand what is going on, consciousness *directly* collapses the quantum function. Without consciousness, there is no collapse. The state vector (i.e., the spectrum of probabilities) remains in potential until consciousness, an observer, actually notices or measures what is going on in the quantum domain. Only then does the state vector—the probabilities—collapse and become an actual event, the building blocks of our actual world. Depending on what we mean by "mediation," it could be meaningful to say, "consciousness mediates the collapse of the wave function." Without consciousness, the collapse from possibility to actuality wouldn't happen.

Perhaps the confusion comes from using the word "measured." Every measurement requires an observation, and so to ask whether consciousness (an observation) "mediates the formation of the measured state vector" is really a tautology. It's really asking: "Does observation mediate the formation of an observation?" The question already contains its own answer: "Yes, of course: Consciousness 'mediates' every measurement."

I guess my real question is—and you're answering it—"in what ways do quantum processes depend on consciousness?"

Well that is probably the greatest mystery confronting modern science. It is a total mystery how consciousness collapses the wave function. Modern science is based on the metaphysics of materialism—the idea that the fundamental nature of reality is pure matter or energy, without any trace of consciousness whatsoever.

Materialists assume that the world began about 13.7 billion years ago in the Big Bang, spewing out lots of very, very hot plasma energy. Then over the eons this energy cooled and evolved, and became more and more complex, forming different kinds of matter like atoms and molecules, and eventually living cells, nervous systems, and brains. Only at that point did consciousness come into being. That, in a nutshell, is the standard story of scientific materialism.

It happens to make no sense whatsoever because it assumes that you can get something non-physical (consciousness) out of a bunch of ingredients that were entirely non-conscious to begin with. That would require a miracle. But miracles are precisely what modern science denies are possible. So, scientific materialism is in the very embarrassing situation of requiring a miracle to be true, and yet it denies the possibility of miracles. In short, for scientific materialism to be true it must be false! That's really an impossible dilemma for any science or philosophy to find itself in. In philosophy, we call it *reductio ad absurdum*—it is reduced to absurdity.

How would you define the irreducible unit? What would that be to you?

Well, I can talk about it in two ways. One would be the quantum, the quantum of action, which is the irreducible element of the physical world. By definition, a quantum is indivisible; it always comes as a whole. That's what the word "quantum" means: a whole packet of action, a packet of energy. That would be the indivisible unit from the perspective of quantum physics.

From the perspective of philosophy, however, I would go along with my favorite philosopher, British metaphysician Alfred North Whitehead, who said that the ultimate indivisible units are *"actual occasions."* What he means is that every moment is a *moment of experience,* and these moments of experience are the fundamental building blocks of reality.

Whitehead has pointed out that every moment lasts for an infinitesimal amount of time, completes itself, and then becomes an expired experience. It becomes an *object* in the past for the next moment of experience in the present. The process of reality, everywhere and at all times, is the moment of now, now, now, collapsing into the past of just a moment ago. The present subject of experience becomes an object in the past, which, in turn, is then experienced by the next new moment of experience. And so reality continues to unfold from moment to moment, with the present becoming the past, and the past streaming into, and informing, the next new moment. That process is the fundamental nature of reality.

The fundamental unit, therefore, is not a thing. It is a unit of time (or space-time). You could think of it as a quantum bubble of space-time. That is the fundamental nature of what is real and actual, and it includes both mind and matter—consciousness and energy—always bundled together into this unit called an actual occasion.

We have kind of touched on the next question, but I need to ask it point blank. Do you think that consciousness is a field, a wave, or both?

I don't think it is either. Back to what I said earlier: only things that exist in space can have the quality or characteristic of a field. A field is something spread out in space, whether it is a field where cows munch away on grass or whether it is an electromagnetic or gravitational field. All fields exist in space. Consciousness doesn't exist in space, and so it cannot be spread out like a field. It isn't a kind of wave, either. A wave, remember, is something that vibrates in space. Consciousness doesn't vibrate in space because it doesn't exist in space.

Vibrations are mechanisms; they are forms of energy moving in space. Mechanisms work by exchanging energy between points in space. Think of the cogs in an old-fashioned clock, ticking off time as the cogwheels turn. That's a mechanism. The gears in your car are another example where energy is transmitted from one point in space to another. That's what a mechanism is. Consciousness doesn't work that way. There is no mechanism of consciousness. Consciousness works by sharing *meaning*, not by exchanging energy.

For example, you and I are having this conversation right now, and hopefully to some extent we understand one another because we understand the meaning being communicated. But that meaning is not traveling through the atmosphere or through the phone line. You can open up a phone line but you will never see any meaning in there. All you will see is a bunch of flowing electrons. Meaning is not something that travels through space. You and I are sharing the meaning of the words. The *sound* of the words is traveling through space as vibrations, but the *meaning* itself is something we share in consciousness. Meaning is something we *feel*. It transcends spatial dimensions.

Do you believe that we have complete free will?

No, not complete. We are determined to a great extent. The fact that we are embodied beings means that a lot of mechanisms determine what is going on in our bodies. Even our minds to a great extent run on habit. For example, beliefs are habits of mind, and most of the time most of us operate according to our belief systems. As long as we are operating from our beliefs, we are not exercising free will or choice. We are operating from habits, sometimes very old habits of mind and old ways of thinking.

We are determined both by the physicality of our bodies and by the physicality of the environment around us. We are determined by our genes, by our nervous systems, by our brains. No doubt about it, determinism pushes us along; the pressure of the past pulsing into the present moment. But that's not the whole story. In addition to the determinism of the past, we also have the spark of spirit in every moment, the creative spark or ability make choices. We are both determined and free. We make choices from among the possibilities that exist in every moment. Every moment is the growing tip of the past, but it comes shrouded in a cloud of possibilities.

Every new moment comes into being not just with the long tail of its past trailing behind, but also sparkling with a halo of new possibilities; otherwise, nothing new could ever happen. This trail from the past (the determinism of the objective physical world) plus the halo of present possibilities (think of quantum waves) are the raw material for consciousness to work with in every moment. Consciousness chooses among those possibilities to introduce something new that happens in the next moment, something that could not have been predicted from the determinism of everything that had happened up to that point. So, yes, we do have free will, and we are also determined.

I think following a spiritual path minimizes the degree to which we are determined both by our belief systems and by our embodiment—a path where we cultivate the ability to make more choices, to realize more possibility. That's one way of understanding spiritual practice: it is a way to shift the ratio between the degree to which we are determined and the degree to which we are free. As long as we are embodied beings, we will always be pushed along by some amount of determinism and yet we always have some choice. Even if we were imprisoned in solitary confinement, we could still choose either to accept where we are and what is happening or choose to resist it. We always have choice.

We have the choice whether or not we react.

Yes we do. It is not always an easy process, but yes we always have that choice.

Even though you have pretty much covered my next question, I want to ask it this way. Imagine you are a two-year-old strapped in the back seat of a car, and you have a little yellow steering wheel. Consciousness, God, Source—whatever you want to call it—is in the front seat driving the car. You come up to a stop sign and the playground is on the right, the grocery store is on the left. Consciousness (God, Source) says, "I am going to the grocery store," and you say, "Oh no, I'm going to the playground." Whose steering wheel is going to work and why? Do we have a choice, here?

Well, if we are the infant in the back seat, we do have a choice. We can choose to try to override the Big Steering Wheel or let it take us where it will.

Is there a potential for that little yellow steering wheel to work?

Yes, we can turn the yellow steering wheel, but it's not going to make the tiniest bit of difference to the direction of the car. We can make choices and our choices can also be embedded in an illusion that they are going to make a difference when they don't. So we can make choices to take action—we do this all the time. We make choices to take certain actions, and often we have the power to take those actions. But sometimes we fall short, too—especially if we are attached to the desire for those actions to produce a particular result. There are no guarantees that our best intentions will always produce the results we want.

To go back to your very interesting metaphor, turning our little yellow steering wheel will lead to the result we want only if it happens to coincide with the direction the real steering wheel turns the car. When we choose to turn the little yellow steering wheel, we are exercising choice, but it's not *our* choice that moves the car. What's really turning the car is the divine or greater consciousness that chooses to turn the steering wheel. Only when our intentions are aligned with the divine intention—the intention or intrinsic intelligence of the cosmos itself—do "our" intentions actually have potency.

So, really, the only free will we have is how we are going to react when we discover we are not going to the playground?

Yes, unless our free will happens to be an expression of the greater will of the cosmos expressing itself through us. There are definitely times when our will makes a difference in the world. At such times we are open to the divine or greater will of the cosmos expressing itself through our little egoic minds. That can, and does, happen. Most of the time, however, the egoic will operates under the illusion that it can actually turn the little yellow steering wheel and make a difference.

Here's a two-part question. From the experiments of Bill Tiller and Robert Jahn (at Princeton), we know that cohesive intention can manipulate physical reality. Given the power of the mind to alter reality, are we in a kind of divine "movie" where everything is pretty much predetermined by Big Mind? Or are we able to get into a very cohesive mental state and subtly manipulate reality? Does that make sense?

I think I know what you are asking, and it's actually in many ways a variation of the question from a moment ago—just a little more sophisticated version of it. The big question here of course—the 64-trillion-dollar question—is, "*Who* makes the choice?"

When we say "I choose," who is this "I" that is choosing? If we spent an hour discussing this—or even a month—I don't think we would have enough time to adequately and sufficiently answer that question. That's the perennial mystery at the heart of spiritual traditions: who is this "I," who is the thinker of "my" thoughts, who is it that makes choices? We can talk about that for a long time, but I don't think we will ever come to any final conclusion. That question is very much like a Zen koan. It is something we need to *live into* rather than give an answer to.

When we ask "who am I?" or "who is it that chooses?" we are turning direct awareness back into itself, and rather than feel compelled to come up with an answer that can be expressed in language, I think we need to engage with that question in a profound way. When we do, it can lead to a kind of transformation, and that in itself becomes the answer. Who we *are* becomes the answer rather than what we *say*.

Very good answer, I like it. Do you think that the conception of self could perhaps be a vast collection of dualities?

Well, yes, every concept is necessarily dualistic, so the concept of "self" is dualistic because it involves the opposite, which is the idea of "no-self." Just because every concept is necessarily dualistic doesn't mean it is bad. Dualistic distinctions are how we actually understand things in language and thought, so I'm not coming down on dualism. But I am interested in finding ways that help us to transcend the dualisms of concepts, and to engage much more in the practice of what I call "sacred silence" where we can get beyond language.

I've done a lot of talking in this interview so far, and I'm very aware that I'm speaking rapidly, trying to get as much information across as possible. However, I think a much more effective way for us to communicate, particularly if we were face to face, would be just to sit together in silence, just be together, and not have to speak, or answer questions. There is a power in silence that is, unfortunately, very alien to our culture, to our society. It is something I would like to see emphasized much more in our educational system—the value and power of just "being" and sitting in silence. Of course, it doesn't have to be *sitting*, it could be walking or running, but the point is to be together in silence.

This world doesn't know how to do that.

Yes, I know. Or, rather, the modern world has forgotten.

I have one more question about how consciousness communicates with the brain. We know the brain doesn't think. I visualize it as some sort of processor, but it has to receive the information from consciousness somehow. Do you think it receives . . . I don't know the word so I am going to use the metaphor . . . Morse code, frequencies, resonance, rat-a-tat-tat, etc.? An intention is asserted by consciousness and the brain receives those signals and interprets what they are, based on the individual's conditioning? Does that make any sense?

Yes. Without a doubt, the brain does play a very significant role in shaping what goes on in our awareness, our consciousness. Using fMRI and PET scans, neuroscience is revealing a great deal about what goes on in the brain when people are in a particular state of consciousness. That can be very useful information. However, it becomes misleading when people think that what they see happening in the brain *is* what is happening in consciousness. That's a very, very mistaken conclusion to jump to. There is no way that what goes on in the brain (which is *physical)* equals what goes on in consciousness (which is *non-physical)*. Nevertheless, it is true that whatever happens in the brain has an effect on what goes on in consciousness and the reverse, of course, is also true: whatever choices we make will show up as events happening in the brain. That is one of the things we can see from fMRIs and PET scans.

One of the more exciting developments in neuroscience during the past couple of decades is the discovery that the brain is actually very malleable; very plastic. This is referred to as neuroplasticity. Up until about twenty years ago, the standard dogma in brain science was that pretty much beyond the age of adolescence the brain was set in stone for the rest of our lives. That was a pretty bleak conclusion. It basically meant that there was no point in trying to change anything about your personality or yourself after the age of 18, 20, or 25. At some point you were set in stone and that was it.

What they have now realized by watching what goes on in the brain is that when people create intentions or exercise choice it actually creates new neural pathways; new parts of the nervous system start to grow, so we can actually change the wiring in the brain to set up new behavior patterns. What we think and what we choose does make a difference to what happens in the brain. That's why psycho-spiritual practices such as affirmations can be effective—because they lay down new neural pathways, new ways the brain operates. We can create new channels for brain activity to flow through, and that can have an effect on our behavior, and back on our consciousness. The possibilities for creating long-lasting transformation through new "virtuous neural circuits" are really exciting. That's one of the areas I'm working on for my next book.

Does the mind think or does it simply know?

The mind does both. Thinking is one way the mind knows things.

How does it think? When we say this, are we talking about Big Mind or little mind?

In this case, I am talking about little mind, our egoic mind.

Let's talk about Big Mind.

Does the Big Mind think? I would say Big Mind thinks through little mind.

Okay. Let's talk about your book, Consciousness from Zombies to Angels. A friend of mine, Gerald Schroeder, wrote a book called The Science of God. Gerald's background is an interesting combination. He was trained in physics at MIT and as a theologian in Israel. In his book, he discusses the first humanoids, the first upright beings with a brain that could think. He says that it lacked a soul. On one page, he would outline the physics and on the next page he would outline the ancient Jewish teachings, comparing the two pieces of information and how they support one another. It made me think of what you talk about in your book. I think that the soul must have come into existence at some point if his work is correct. I don't know. Do you think those types of beings still exist?

No, I don't. In *Consciousness from Zombies to Angels* I talk about what I call "philosophical zombies," and these are just imaginary creatures that don't actually exist. The idea is that a philosophical zombie is a creature just like a human being in every physical respect. It has blood and bones and nervous systems and brains exactly like ours. It bleeds if cut . . . .

That's exactly what he said, and he said it was in the Talmud if I am not mistaken.

Yes and so playing with the idea of "philosophical zombies" is a thought experiment. They are exactly like us in every *physical* respect, but they have no minds, no feeling, no awareness, no sentience; no consciousness whatsoever. They are "zombies" because nobody's home. But such beings don't actually exist . . . .

Don't now or never have?

Never have, according to my understanding of the nature of reality. Remember, earlier in our conversation, I said that the ground of being is consciousness and energy? That means there never was a time when there wasn't consciousness and there never was a time when there wasn't some kind of embodiment. Whether we go back a million years, or three millions years, or a billion years, or even back to the Big Bang, there was still some consciousness present. There was still some ability to feel and to make choices all the way back, and all the way down. That is the only way we can make sense of the fact that today we are made up cells that are made of molecules that are made of atoms that are made of subatomic particles that are made of quanta or quarks or superstrings or whatever lies at the deepest level of physical reality. Whatever it is, all the way down, there has to be some degree of consciousness at every level, otherwise it is a complete mystery to explain how come we are made of that stuff and yet we are bodies that can think, feel and make choices.

The only way to account to the fact that we as embodied beings can think, feel, and make choices is to assume that at every level of everything that constitutes us—our cells, our molecules our atoms, our subatomic particles—there must be some degree of choice and consciousness there, too. There never was a time where there was some being made up of matter that didn't have some degree of consciousness. As far as I can tell, that idea is incoherent. It makes no sense whatsoever to think that there could be beings that didn't have some degree of consciousness or ensoulment.

In Consciousness from Zombies to Angels, you talk about electrons being conscious. Did you just choose electrons over protons and neutrons? Also, if an electron is conscious and we know that electrons have mass—that means even a rock is conscious to some degree. Right?

Well, yes and no. Here's where it is important to make another philosophical distinction. Making fine distinctions is the business of philosophers. So I would say that all the molecules that make up a rock have their own degree of molecular consciousness, and all the atoms in those molecules have some degree of atomic consciousness. But the rock, *as a rock,* does not have "rock consciousness" the way a human being has human consciousness or a bat or a bird has bat or bird consciousness.

A rock is just a collection of individual molecules that don't have any unified coherence the way the cells in living organisms do. Living organisms are made up of parts that form themselves into a cohesive unit, and therefore they experience unified consciousness. A rock, by contrast, is just a heap. It's just a bunch of molecules squashed together, and the rock does not have any unit coherence. I would say a rock *as a rock* doesn't experience rock consciousness, but that there is consciousness in the molecules that make up the rock. So, when people claim to have communication with a rock I don't have any difficulty accepting that as a plausible description of their experience. I would say they are actually communicating with the sentience in the molecules of that rock.

Do you ever hear a high-pitched noise in your head—a high-pitched frequency? You might think of it as tinnitus.

I think I probably have . . . maybe after a very loud rock concert.

No not that kind of noise. Have you ever been out in the woods where it is so silent that it is screaming?

Ah! Yes, I have experienced that.

Okay. One thing I have learned is that every single luminary I have interviewed that has actually had a spiritual epiphany, they have all heard that sound. Ervin Laszlo said it is B flat. Do you know Ervin? He's a child prodigy in music and so he knows his sounds, and he said "Eva, it is B flat," which, interestingly, is the frequency of silence in hertz and also the sound that comes from black holes. So I think it is very interesting that we all have that sound when we become conscious.

There is also a physiological aspect I think . . . linguistics is a problem here . . . our resonance is much faster and it burns up magnesium. You know magnesium is highly flammable, and magnesium deficiency can cause tinnitus, so I think it's a good thing and a bad thing at the same time. I've noticed that when I meditate on that "sound things" happen a lot quicker, so it makes me wonder if it's the frequency of the original intention for things to start happening in the universe.

CHAPTER 3

Dean Radin, Ph.D.

Dean Radin is senior scientist at the Institute of Noetic Sciences (IONS) and adjunct faculty in the Department of Psychology at Sonoma State University. His original career track as a concert violinist shifted into science after earning a BSEE degree in electrical engineering, *magna cum laude* in physics, from the University of Massachusetts, Amherst, and then an MS in electrical engineering and a Ph.D. in psychology from the University of Illinois, Urbana-Champaign. For a decade he worked on advanced telecommunications research and development at AT&T Bell Laboratories and GTE Laboratories. For over two decades he has been engaged in consciousness research. Before joining the research staff at IONS in 2001, he held appointments at Princeton University, University of Edinburgh, University of Nevada, and several Silicon Valley think-tanks, including Interval Research Corporation and SRI International, where he worked on a classified program investigating psychic phenomena for the U.S. government. He is author or coauthor of over 200 technical and popular articles, a dozen book chapters, and several books including *The Conscious Universe* and *Entangled Minds* which have been translated into six foreign languages. His technical articles have appeared in journals ranging from *Foundations of Physics* and *Physics Essays* to *Psychological Bulletin* and *Journal of Consciousness Studies*; he was featured in a *New York Times Magazine* article; and he has appeared on dozens of television shows ranging from the BBC's *Horizon* and PBS's *Closer to Truth* to *Oprah* and *Larry King Live*. He has given over 200 interviews and talks, including invited presentations at Harvard, Stanford, Cambridge, and Princeton, for industries including Google and Johnson & Johnson, and for government organizations including the U.S. Navy and DARPA. In 2010, he spent a month lecturing in India as the National Visiting Professor of the Indian Council of Philosophical Research, a program in the Indian government's Ministry of Human Resource Development.

Eva: Dean, please tell us a little bit about yourself.

Dean: I'm originally trained as a classical violinist, and in college I switched to electrical engineering, and in graduate school I switched again into psychology. So I have an undergraduate and a master's degree in electrical engineering and doctorate in psychology from the University of Illinois, in Champagne.

We can acquaint ourselves with your work through your book, Entangled Minds: Extra Sensory Experiences in a Quantum Reality, and also in the film, What the Bleep: Down the Rabbit Hole.

Yes, Down the Rabbit Hole.

What is your participation in the film?

I was interviewed for maybe eight hours or so, and they added this as a new segment, because *What the Bleep* had been expanded, like a director's cut. Part of the expansion was to address some of the questions people had about the first movie about the nature of the evidence itself. So they filmed an experiment in our lab here at the Institute of Noetic Sciences and they interviewed me about it afterwards.

Which one of your experiments was it?

This was an experiment looking at our laboratory analogue of distant healing. We generally don't do clinical healing research in our lab here because we're not equipped for it, but what we can do is look at how one person's intention will influence or be detected by another person at a distance. We see that as a physiological change rather than as a healing response. So that's the experiment that we did.

What was the general receptivity of it?

The general public has always found these ideas interesting, because the raw experience—I'm talking here of psychic experiences or mystical experiences and even in some cases, religious epiphanies—are very common. People have these things all the time, so movies and books that talk about these things tend to be accepted pretty readily by the public.

What about responses from your colleagues?

In science, it's a completely different issue. It's almost as if there are two separate cultures. It isn't the case that scientists don't have these experiences, because they do, but within the scientific culture, much of what is considered to be acceptable to talk about is driven by *theory*. So at the present time, we don't really have good theories to explain why people would have these experiences, and because we don't have the theories, it becomes a taboo topic within science.

But if they can actually see that it happens, why do they not believe it?

Because an explanation, or a theory, in a sense it trumps data. Now, it shouldn't do that. All scientists would probably agree that data and observation should always override theory. In fact, in the history of science that has always been the case, eventually. It is always the data that forces the theory to change. But it is just a natural consequence of people falling in love with their theory. You know, we all have stories that we tell ourselves about the way we think the world works. People tend to fall in love with those stories and anything which counters the story is perceived as an attack.

So data which don't fit the theory are expelled in the same way, as though you are being physically attacked.

Do you have some new information in this book that is different from The Conscious Universe?

This book is an update. There is almost ten years of additional data and like any other area of science, the amount of data being produced is increasing exponentially over time. So there is a lot of additional data to talk about. I also talk about some new types of experiments that I couldn't talk about in the first book.

Can you tell us a little bit about the new data, before we get started on the consciousness portion?

Ok . . . I'm actually kind of uncomfortable being put in a position of authority, because Einstein once said, the universe punished his disdain for authority by making him one. I'm in that same position because after studying this realm for 25 years or so, I've learned what I actually don't understand. I have a good sense of what we understand, but a much greater sense of all that's left to be learned. And I know that there are no authorities in this realm.

It's your humility that matters when it comes to that.

Well, perhaps that's what it is, but nevertheless, the idea of being asked questions and giving an authoritative response is not part of my nature. So anyway, one new type of experiment that has appeared recently is because of the rise of the Internet. We can now do experiments where we are no longer looking, as we did in the past, at an individual person's experience, or sometimes a couple's experience, but instead what I call collective psi. We look at psychic experiences in the collective, meaning hundreds of thousands to millions of people. The way we do this is through experiments on the web—some of which have attracted 80 million trials from a third of a million people all around the world.

Some of them you can reach through the web page of IONS—*www.noetic.org*—and others are at another site I wrote called Got Psi, which is a take-off on the milk commercial, got milk—*www.*

gotpsi.org—and both of these sites have similar experiments. The idea is that most of the experiments are just for entertainment, but we also use the data for research in that we can see how the performance on these tests change over time. These are very simple online card tests, where you see five cards and you have to select the one that you think the computer will select immediately after your choice. So it's essentially a precognition test; can you guess the right card. You make your selection and you see what the computer does and then you get immediate feedback. When you finish a run of 25 cards you see how your performance compared to everybody else on that day.

Readers can have lots of fun with that, if they visit the site. Now, moving more directly into our interview . . . my questions for you are all about consciousness and power of intent and free will. My sense of the word "consciousness" is that it's too general to be particularly useful, so I'd love for you to share your definition of consciousness.

I think of it as anything having to do with the mind. So, that would include conscious awareness, which is the opposite of coma, but it also includes the unconscious because we know the brain and mind is always engaged in unconscious processing. It includes things like memory and the production of imagery, cognition in the sense of information processing, and so on. But because of evidence from parapsychology, it also includes the possibility that mind extends in space and time in a way that the brain cannot. So consciousness then is part of the spectrum which is brain-like processing on the one hand, and far beyond that on the other. My own research has focused on the "beyond" part of consciousness.

What is your definition of mind? Do you think that mind is contained within consciousness or are they one and the same?

It's the same definition that I just gave. One way to make a distinction though is typically to say, do you think that mind and the brain are identically the same? And I would respond by saying no, they are not identical.

Would you say the brain thinks, or that it simply processes?

Well, thinking is a kind of processing. We can't deny the evidence from neuroscience, which provides very strong evidence that the brain is a kind of organic computer. It does compute. Large portions of the brain are engaged in keeping the body alive and computing what's called "anticipatory computing," where some portion of the brain/mind is constantly in trying to figure out what comes next. This makes sense from an evolutionary point of view from any organism. You always have to be anticipating what is happening. So, the brain is kind of a living computer, but standard neuroscience would say that that's all there is, and that's where we part company. Because I think there is a lot more.

What would be "a lot more"?

A lot more is that the brain and the mind are not the same thing. So, the mind is clearly associated with the brain, it is deeply influenced by it and vice versa. But the mind has capabilities that we don't understand yet in terms of brain function. If, say, clairvoyance is true, and I believe the data says that it is, then how does the brain get information which is located somewhere else? The physical brain is tightly located inside your head and it's not entirely clear how, by any obvious physical means that information at a distance, beyond the reach of the ordinary senses, and even worse, at a distance in time, could get inside your head so that you can perceive it? This has been *the* fundamental problem, the challenge presented by these phenomena for science. How does the information get into your head? Somehow the mind can do these things, whereas the brain cannot.

I believe that we are all one with everything; do you believe that our individual mind would be contained within our electromagnetic field or aura?

Well, if the mind is one with everything, then it's not located anywhere.

It would be that irreducible unit, I guess.

Right. So, I tend to think of mind as located everywhere, and everyone is extended in space and time. This doesn't make any sense at all from a common sense perspective, but neither does most of modern physics make sense from a common sense perspective. The fact is what our senses provide to us is a very, very limited slice of the fabric of reality. I believe our minds have the capability of experiencing a larger portion of that fabric than our eyes and ears can.

You are familiar with David Hawkins1 work, right? What would your reason be that there exists eleven levels, but regardless of the number of levels, what would you think the reason being for the various levels of awareness that people have? When I say awareness, I mean some people absolutely refuse to believe that psychic phenomena exists and others think that it might and other people are absolutely convinced that it exists. It affects the way they interpret information that they receive from the world. What would be the reason people have different levels of awareness?

You could ask why are some people talented at the piano and others can't play at all? The answer is there are natural tendencies and temperaments that people have. Where they come from is partially genetics, partially what you are exposed to as a child, and who knows what else. Talent just arises, and so it is in this realm as well.

Take something simple, like basic temperament. In terms of the Myers Briggs Type Inventory, based on Jungian psychological types, there are sixteen possible cells in this personality test. The highest frequency of people's experience and belief in psychic phenomena is also the same cell that has the fewest number of people

---

1 Sir David R. Hawkins, M.D., Ph.D. is a nationally renowned psychiatrist, physician, researcher, spiritual teacher and lecturer. The uniqueness of his contribution to humanity comes from the advanced state of spiritual awareness known as "Enlightenment." A trademark of Dr. Hawkins's research is his pioneering, internationally-known and applied "Map of Consciousness," presented in the ever-popular book Power vs. Force (1995). The "Map of Consciousness" incorporates findings from quantum physics and nonlinear dynamics thereby confirming the classical "stages" of spiritual evolution found in the world's sacred literature as actual "attractor fields."

in it. So, this one cell (type) in Myers Briggs terms is known as INFJ—introverted, intuitive, feeling, and judging are the words used to describe it. It includes something like 4 percent of the population. Among people in that cell, almost everyone either has experiences of, or somehow intuitively knows, that psychic effects are real. And yet, this means that 96 percent of the rest of the population has a completely different temperament and they either don't accept it at all, or they do, but not to the same degree. So, here we're simply talking about personality differences among people. You take the combination of personality, talent, training, and exposure to experience, and it's not so surprising that you can end up with a pretty large spectrum of belief about these things.

What about people who, for lack of a better description, become spontaneously enlightened and suddenly "understand"? I had that experience, and suddenly left the fundamental southern Baptist belief system, within 24 hours, and spontaneously understood the concept of I AM, without any kind of conditioning from anywhere.

Where those transformative experiences come from is a real mystery. We have a project here at IONS looking at the nature of transformation to try and understand how it is that, in a flash, someone can become different. This is a major challenge by the way, within psychology and psychiatry because most models in psychiatry for example, it is thought that the basic personality is set very early on in life and does not change. Well we know that is not completely true because people do have experiences like your own in which your whole worldview can change pretty dramatically.

In an instant too.

Yes. My guess is that it's not that the world at large has changed at all, it's more that your perception or sense of self changes. I think psychic phenomena are oftentimes thought of as something like a cosmic hiccup, in the sense that it's a small cluster of weird things that happen to people. But that's not the case at all. Psychic phenomena are part of the spectrum of human experiences. On one end you have things that are extremely mundane, like the feeling of being stared at; I believe that is a type of psychic experience. At the other end of that same spectrum, you have a religious epiphany or mystical sense of union. They all can be mapped out on this same spectrum of something having to do with your experience of the holistic fabric of reality, the way that it actually is, rather than the way that common sense presents it.

Do you think that maybe consciousness is a field, and suddenly somehow your frequency raises or changes to a different frequency and that information could be encoded in time space intervals and something occurs that unlocks the door to something that has additional and different knowledge? Could that be an explanation?

Well, it is one explanation. And as you said, the language that we use is not quite precise enough yet to have an explanation that everyone is going to be happy with. I understand why terms like frequency are used because internally it feels something like that.

Something shifts; have you had that happen?

I have had miniature versions of that, yes.

It feels different, something happens. What could make that happen?

We don't know. That's why we do research to try and figure it out. Of course, a related thing is when people have very strong energetic experiences, where they feel they are connected to a battery. But so far, it's been exceptionally difficult to find any kind of instrument that we have that would measure what that is. So, the truth is, we don't know yet what these things are, but not knowing of course, is quite different that simply observing that it exists. This is really where the controversy in science is still stuck, on the question of existence.

Personally, I get numbers in my head for people; it's like a machine I have. If I get a number for you, it'll be a different number than I get for other people. It'll be close, but it will be some number off. I think that what I'm hearing is frequencies of organs and I'm wondering if consciousness could be the reason that everyone's frequency—or the number I "get" that I interpret as frequency—would be different with everyone because everyone has a different level of consciousness. By that I mean, their awareness of everything that is, not just being awake.

It could be that, but it could also be because their bodies are very different. Physical structure, the DNA, everything, is very different from one person to the next. So maybe that's what it is.

Could we describe the organs as having frequencies and oscillations?

Well, it is true that virtually every physical object, whether a living cell or a rock, does have resonant frequencies, bit whether that's related to the numbers that you are getting or not, is unknown.

What do you believe to be the source of creativity and intentionality?

These are two quite different things. The source of creativity includes some mundane reasons, like if you study a lot you tend to be more creative because you have more knowledge available to think of something new. But the breakthrough insights that people get seem to come from the same place that telepathy and clairvoyance come from. When you read the stories of the great inventors, they all sound similar in the sense that they have a dream, or they will go into a reverie and the whole answer to the problem they're working on will just fall out of the sky.

It doesn't come in bits and pieces, it comes all at once.

It comes all at once. And now the challenge is how to take this amazing vision that they received and turn it into something. So that's where I think genius level creative insight comes from: the "beyond" side of our consciousness. Intention is something different. It is simply, in a crass sense, desire. It is a wish or a purpose and every organism has a certain goal whether it is simply to exist or to eat or to do some other thing. We can also think of intention in a much more refined manner, where we don't simply have goals to exist and to maintain the body, but we may have more subtle goals having to do with life plans and wishes and that sort of thing.

You've done a great deal of research on intention. Tell us a little bit about . . . in some of your experiments, when you placed intentions on the random event generator, how quickly does it happen? When, for example, you tell all the balls to fall to the left, how long does it take that to occur?

It doesn't take any time at all. Since some aspect of the mind is extended in both space and time, it's tempting to say, well, if you are thinking about random bits or coins or something, then in two milliseconds the system begins to respond. But that's not how it is. A system will respond in a way that is timeless, and here is where we are going to have a problem with language again. The reason I am mentioning this is because there have been many, many experiments looking at the role of precognition in both experiments involving intention and other kinds of experiments, and it's very clear that we do have access to future information, and we also have access to information in the past that we weren't aware of before. So as soon as we open the possibility that mind extends through time, then asking questions like how fast does this occur assumes that we are dealing with some sort of fixed time. And that's not how the phenomenon works, nor is it clear that "fixed time" is a real quantity.

How do they work?

We still don't know very well, but we do know from the data we get in experiments that to think of this in terms of ordinary causation—you know, like billiard balls hitting other billiard balls, or like gears in a clock—that that explanation is insufficient to describe how these phenomena work. It's something different than that; something bigger.

I asked that question because so many people don't believe this. There's so much evidence out there, but the average person doesn't understand the scientific language, or the format it's presented in, or they just don't want to believe it. But you've proven that intent is real and that effects happen. So I'm wondering, why can't I manifest a car in front of me right now? Is it that the intention is not clear, or I'm not including the longitude and latitude in my "order," and it is manifesting in bits and pieces strewn around, and I have to go and find it?

I would say that intention does seem to push the world around a little bit, but the world also has an enormous amount of inertia in it. If you want to push the world in such a way that a car will magically appear on your doorstep, a large number of things have to occur in order to make that happen. It's not going to simply assemble itself out of molecules in the air and appear. That's not going to happen. But there could be a chain of events that might occur, each one relatively minor, and after, say, 10,000 of these minor events the event would happen.

So it would be important to pay attention to those synchronicities that happen?

Not only that, but there's the consideration that world has its own needs and inertia. There's a lot of people out there all holding their own intentions, and the world sort of cranks along like a large heavy truck. You could stand next to a truck and try to push it and it's not going to move very much. But if you stood in the right place and the brake was off and you pushed real hard for a long time, it would begin to move. So when people have a wish for something mundane like a car to appear, and it's not appearing in ten minutes, one possibility is that they just haven't pushed hard enough for long enough.

Are experiments as effective with a few people as they are with a lot of people? The power of intention (emphasis added: intention = prayer) . . . does it matter how many you have to focus on something?

We don't know yet about how many. There is fairly good evidence that suggests that some people are much better at this than others. So again, it has something to do with talent and probably a lot to do with practice.

Does it have anything to do with one's level of consciousness?

Well, again recognizing that our language is inadequate here, an answer could be a qualified yes. It has something to do with levels of consciousness but it's not too much different than saying that it has something to do with a level of talent combined with practice. So talent, the level of consciousness and talent, it may be those are all synonymous.

How many people did you use to conduct your random event generator? For people that don't know what that is, please tell us a bit about that.

For a simple experiment, imagine you have a coin flipper. It's a device that simply produces the electronic equivalent of heads and tails, and it does it automatically. It's an electronic circuit and the source of the randomness that determines the head or tail can be traced down into quantum events. The important component in these devices is called a Zener diode, and it produces events called tunneling, which is a quantum phenomenon. Ultimately, these microscopic events are turned into sequences not of heads and tails but of zeros and ones, in a random order.

In an experiment, you might have somebody press a button. The random generator would produce 200 bits, and you would ask the person to try and make it produce more ones than zeros. It is as simple as that. By chance you would expect one hundred ones. If the random generator produced 200 bits, you would be successful if you produced 110 or 120 ones at any given trial. But you'd have to do this repeatedly in an experiment. This kind of experiment has been done with many variations for about fifty years now, and there are about six hundred experiments that have been done by dozens of investigators and thousands of participants in the experiments. Overall, it shows that if you are wishing for ones, the machines tend to produce ones. If you are wishing for zeros, it tends to produce that too, and under controlled conditions when nobody is wishing anything, it tends to behave along the lines of what you would expect by chance.

What about the one where the ping pong balls fell down into the slot? How many people focused on that?

I think you are referring to the random mechanical cascade, which is at Princeton University. That had something like 5,000 polyethylene balls that would fall down a shoot and then hit a bunch of pegs. It was designed in such a way that it would create a bell shape curve at the bottom after hitting all these pegs. The person's goal would be to try to shift the distribution of the balls slightly to the right or slightly to the left. I don't know exactly how many trials were done, probably tens of thousands, and the results showed that the direction that you wish the balls to be moved, they tended to behave in that way.

Would it be one person at a time focusing on it?

Mostly one person at a time?

It's amazing that one person can do that.

Well, one person may be able to do it to a very small degree and the only reason you are able to see it is because there are tens of thousands of trials. All of these effects in these studies tend to be very small but there is so much data now that we can say with high confidence that the effects are real even though they are small.

If the effects are small with one person, would they be greater with a greater number of people? I guess what I'm saying here is if that's true, if one person thinks peace in the world and a little bit of peace occurs, if a lot of people thought it at the same time, then we would have a great amount of peace come all of a sudden?

Yes, but with an important caveat. The caveat is that these effects behave much more like wave-like structures than they do particles.

Can you please elaborate?

Let's go back to the idea of trying to push a truck. An individual can push a truck a little bit. If you had 100 people helping you push, it would go a lot better. So you can simply say if you have one person, you have one unit of force, and if you have 100 people, you have 100 units of force. Unfortunately, that doesn't appear to be the way that these phenomena work. They work more like waves on a pond. You can drop two pebbles in a pond and the ripples will completely overlap each other. Two points on the pond will have rippling waves, but the waves will penetrate or pass right through each other. So, if you have a large pond and you want to get all of the water out of the pond, you could take a rock and throw it into the pond and a little bit of water would be pushed out as a result. So you might think, well, I'll just get 1,000 friends and we'll all throw our rocks into the pond and it will make all the water spill out. Well, that probably won't happen. The reason is that unless you all throw the rocks in at exactly the same time and at exactly the right configuration, you won't end up with one giant wave. Instead, you will end up with just a very disturbed surface of a pond because all the waves are interfering with each other.

By the same token, if you have one person thinking about peace, that probably does affect the world, a little bit. But if you have 100 people thinking the same thing, if they are not all in exact alignment with each other, then you won't get 100 times more intention. You may end up with zero intention because the waves can cancel each other out.

That makes perfect sense. Let's touch on a topic I know very little about: entities. I've heard people say, an entity got into that person and made them behave in a certain way and you should have seen it when we made it go out. You think that really exists? Or do you think it is something within the person's mind that's caused some force to occur?

You're talking about something like possession. I guess I could accept it in principle, and the reason I say this is because when you look at phenomena like telepathy for example, there is a lot of evidence suggesting that thoughts that arise are certainly mostly your own thoughts, but they're not exclusively your own thoughts. That's the whole point of a telepathy test. Sometimes things can arise in your mind and you don't know where they are coming from. They feel like they are you, but they're not necessarily from you. Those thoughts can be because somebody else is intending that you pick up something from one of their thoughts.

This then raises a question about who is the "self?" Who is the person inside your head? The answer is not so clear. Of course, it's very clear from a traditional neuroscience point of view; the brain is what you are and it's in your head and that's all there is to it. But, psychic phenomena challenges that assumption by suggesting some aspect of the self, of who you think you are, is actually more about a relationship to the rest of the world. So, in principle, there could be a very powerful influence that might disrupt who you think you are and in fact, it's not coming from inside you, it's coming from outside somewhere. So, that's why I say in principle I can accept such a thing. Whether it is ever as powerful as sometimes portrayed, literally a possession, I'm not so sure about that.

Do you believe that the soul is contained in, or consists of, an electromagnetic field of some sort?

I'm not entirely sure what the soul means, but my guess is no. If I interpret the soul as something like a self with a large "S," then in that case I expect it's probably not electromagnetic. At least not electromagnetic in the sense of what we usually think of as electromagnetism and four space (three dimensions of space and one of time). It's probably much, much more complicated than that.

Do you think that knowledge is encoded within frequencies?

That depends on what you mean by frequencies.

I'll provide a little background to explain. I get these numbers in my head and I also see something pulsing. Rollin McCraty said that information is encoded within frequencies it's just a matter of learning the time and spacing between the coding. So, we have this electromagnetic aura, or electromagnetic field—whatever you want to call the aura that you see—and there is some kind of buzzing that goes on within it and information is carried through it, I think. I believe that one day we will be able to test this field and obtain what I call a frequency number. We will know if this field is buzzing at a particular rate, then this person is going to have a kidney disorder, for example. It's just a matter of figuring out what that timing is in between the pulses. Does that make any sense? Do you think that is possible?

Yeah, I mean especially if you imagine that we live in a holographic universe. A hologram basically just consists of frequencies and patterns and reality as we experience it is the hologram playing out. So, if you have the ability to see the hologram itself, as opposed to something that the hologram is playing, then you would probably get a very different sense of what things are made of. You would get a more basic, more fundamental look at what i0.s forming something, especially when it comes to something like the human body. I suppose you would be able to see patterns that had not yet manifested in someone.

There are various healing machines, like Rife, that have to be set to some kind of numbers. A lot of them oscillate at what they call 80,000 hertz. If you're setting that machine for a particular illness or organ, let's say the liver . . . what happens if, say, the liver vibrates at 33,572 and the machine is set at 80,000 hertz. What happens to the energy, since energy doesn't stop it just changes forms, what happens to the energy beyond 33,572 and 80,000 what would happen to that? Where would it go?

It probably wouldn't do anything in the body. It would probably just pass right through.

It wouldn't bother the frequency of any of the other organs?

Well, anything that resonates with 80,000-hertz frequency would absorb that frequency and that would absorb the energy of it, if we are talking about the way that ordinary energy resonates. So, in other words, it is similar to asking a question about a radio. You have a radio turned to a certain dial, what's happening to all of the other stations? They are all there, but it just passes right through.

My last question involves free will. I personally don't believe we have complete free will. If we did, then you could guarantee me that tomorrow you would meet me at Starbucks at 3:00. This is another area I think is really gray. People always say we have free will to do this or that. I think we have free will to place intention, but I don't think we really have complete free will, because if we did, you could tell me that you would meet me at Starbucks tomorrow at 3:00 and you would be there exactly at 3:00, not 5 minutes before or 5 minutes after. I think that if Source, or God if you want to call it, doesn't want you to be there at 3:00, for whatever reason, you won't be there at 3:00. Do you have an opinion about that?

Well, you may have free will and still not be able to make a 3:00 appointment, but for many, many reasons. Free will doesn't mean that you have control of all possible future states. You see, I can intend that I have free will and intend to meet you at 3:00, but maybe transportation is not available. Maybe there is a storm; a million things could happen in between. But that didn't change my original wish. As it turns out, I agree with you that the degree to which we have free will is much less than people think. I think that we do have some capability of making our own decisions and that is where the free will is. But to a very large extent the decisions that we make, the habits that we have, where we live, what we think (all of these things are very strongly embedded in us from upbringing, our genetics, our culture, and so on) they determine to a very large extent what it is that we actually end up doing.

This may be something you do not have the ability to research, but do you think past and future events happen in the past or future, or is everything happening at one time in the hologram? Perhaps in different frequencies of time and space?

If we imagine that there is some existence that is not locked into space and time in the way that we ordinarily experience it, then the answer is yes. It's all there. It's the typical way that someone might describe a mystical experience, in that they perceive the perfect unity of the whole thing. The whole shebang is laid out. The reason why this is difficult to imagine in an ordinary state of awareness is that is certainly not the way that we experience the world, and yet in the right frame of mind, or in the right circumstances, it all fits together perfectly nicely as a single completed entity. In that state, there are no longer concepts of time and space in the usual way.

If you go all the way to the quantum level, does matter really exist?

The further down you go, the more it begins to look like energy and probably the further down from that you go, the more it starts looking like information. But is there matter? Sure, at the level of common sense everyday reality, we certainly encounter matter all the time. Everything is mostly matter in fact.

But on the quantum level, it's not really, is it?

At the quantum level, there aren't "things" in the sense that we experience it in the everyday world. There are no particles, there are no waves, there is no energy, there is nothing like what we experience it in the ordinary sense. So, that's one of the great mysteries in modern physics. The description of the world at the sub-microscopic level or subatomic level is radically different than what common sense shows us, and as a result we quite literally do not have language that can describe what that is like. The best we can do is to provide mathematical equations that tell us what we would expect to see if we did such and such an experiment. We know the equations are quite good, but in terms in what it would be like to shrink down in size below an atom and experience that world, it would be extremely bizarre.

Do you think that consciousness is the irreducible unit?

That's a good question. My guess, and of course this is only a guess, is that mind is in some respects more fundamental than energy or matter. It may be that the core fundamental is actually information and that's the world that mind comes out of—a kind of informational world. There is some historical data that clairvoyants were able to describe certain atomic structures long before there were electron microscopes, and if all that is true then perhaps the mind is able to shrink down below the subatomic realm and describe it. That's why I have a sense that the mind in some ways is more fundamental in what we ordinarily think of as fundamental physics.

CHAPTER 4

Amit Goswami, Ph.D.

Amit Goswami is a retired professor of physics at the University of Oregon, Eugene, Oregon where he served for over thirty years. He is a pioneer of the new paradigm of science called science within consciousness. He is the author of the highly successful textbook *Quantum Mechanics,* the *Quantum Activist Workbook, Physics of the Soul, How Quantum Activism Can Save Civilization, The Self Aware Universe, Creative Evolution, The Visionary Window, God is Not Dead,* and *Quantum Doctor. He also* appears in the movies *What the Bleep Do We know?, The Dalai Lama Renaissance*, and the recently released award-winning documentary, *The Quantum Activist.*

Eva: Before we delve into the topic of consciousness, could you tell us a little bit about yourself?

Amit: Well, I am a physicist, which is of course the first surprise because ordinarily one does not associate a physicist with any wisdom about consciousness.

You've also produced a documentary to help make the essence of your work accessible to the masses.

Yes, the documentary (on DVD) is about my work in quantum activism, and what that entails. It is called *The Quantum Activist,* and serves as an introduction to the new paradigm of science that is developing. It is a way out of the crisis that we have created. There is a crisis of confidence in our science and our worldviews. The crisis is in how we view ourselves. I am pleased with the documentary. When I first watched it in Seattle at the opening, I was amazed. At the end I was feeling enthusiastic about all of this, which surprised me.

I felt the same way. I believe as you do, but being able to watch and hear someone with credentials such as yours made me enthusiastic as well.

In the tail end of the 20th century we found that quantum physics cannot be understood without introducing consciousness squarely into the subject of its interpretation. So, that's how I became involved in consciousness research. Before that, I confess I was an absolute materialist and believed that everything was made of atoms and elementary particles. It was my belief that there was nothing but matter, and consciousness was a brain phenomenon. But if you analyze quantum physics with that idea, you fall flat on your face. You get paradoxes that cannot be resolved.

So upon worrying a few years over these paradoxes, an insight suddenly came to me one day while talking to someone who people would ordinarily refer to as a mystic. While talking to this mystic it occurred to me that if consciousness is the ground of being instead of matter, as is commonly assumed in conventional science, then the paradoxes of quantum physics can all be resolved. Furthermore, there is nothing contradictory about building a science on this new metaphysics.

This is what I found to be extremely surprising and very illuminating. We have been assuming all this time that without the materialist assumption we cannot do science. I found that this is just not true. We have been missing half of our reality in terms of getting and providing scientific explanation because we have held on to this materialist dogma. But if we give that dogma up in favor of the metaphysics of the primacy of consciousness, then this other half of reality—our subjective experiences, consciousness, love, spirituality, and God—can all be included within the purview of science.

What is your definition of consciousness? I ask because of a con-
versation I once had with a medical doctor. I don't know what prompt-
ed me, but I asked, "What is your definition of consciousness?" He
looked at me like I was crazy and said, "The opposite of being in a
coma." And at that moment I realized—oh my—we are warring in the
world because people are having conversations without a meeting of
the minds over terminology, and they aren't even aware they're not
speaking the same language.

Yes. Well, of course for him, awareness and consciousness is
synonymous, even after a hundred years of Freud. So this particular
doctor has never read any psychoanalytic literature, or, if he has,
has not understood any of it. Because how could unconsciousness
be validated if consciousness is not present, if one is in a coma.
Consciousness never goes away. It's that we become unaware. So
what Freud really meant is that there is a distinction between
awareness and unawareness. Both are states of consciousness. In
one state we have a subject/object split; we have an experience. But
that other state makes things happen in the state in which we do
have awareness. In psychoanalysis, we find out what those things
are that bother us in our unconscious that we need to find out in
order to be mentally well functioning.

Consciousness, in my book, is one of those qualities you don't
try to define . . . immediately, at least. We are aware of some aspects
of consciousness; that's all we can do. Because consciousness is the
ground of all being, any definition that you give will fall short.
Consciousness is everything there is. And so, anything that you
use for definition will fall short because it is a phenomenon of consciousness, rather than the other way around. Having said that,
I was writing about consciousness and creativity just today, and
I was writing that materialists make consciousness into linguistic
operational stuff.

Consciousness in their view is just a word that we use to signify
a language use mainly. We have subjects and predicates in our language. I give examples of the Hopi language where there is no subject and object; it is only verbs. That way we don't need to assume
that there is any consciousness. This is a worldview today and we

don't have to quibble about all this at the moment. Today we are in a situation where we can experimentally verify the worldview. One worldview is of course the materialist worldview which everybody knows—scientific materialism. Everything is matter and manifestation of material interaction.

Now this is the thing: material interaction comes with some properties. One property is that all interactions, all communications use signals going through space and time. Another property is that all material interactions are continuous so phenomena have to be continuous according to scientific materialism. The work that we, quantum physicists, are doing suggests that we cannot understand quantum physics without introducing consciousness into it. Not only consciousness but a causally potent consciousness. Quantum physics says that objects are possibilities. How do possibilities become actual events when an observer looks at this possibility? Because the observer never sees possibilities; the observer sees actuality.

How does observation convert possibilities into actualities? This becomes complex because John Von Neumann, a very famous scientist, proved a theorem of mathematics that material interactions can only convert possibilities into other possibilities, never actualities. So consciousness must have a non-material component and to make a long story short, the only paradox interpretation you can give is to suggest that consciousness is the ground of all being and material possibilities are possible because of consciousness itself. Since consciousness is choosing from itself, it does not require any signal. In other words, the new view of this kind of causation is signal-less communication, which is technically called non-local.

Now you have an experimental verifiable consequence. Material interactions start locally, requiring signals, and this new interaction—consciousness interacting with the world—requires no signals; non-local communication. What do the experiments say? Experiments since 1982 are saying that there are indeed non-local interactions in the world, so scientific materialism is ruled out experimentally. Instead, we have experimentally established the idea that a new kind of interaction exists in the world . . . a new kind of ability of communication called downward causation and this is a causal ability of consciousness. We choose from quantum possibilities the actual experience that we have.

Do we choose this in the moment, or is what is happening at this moment something that we chose or created two years ago, or whenever?

Well we have a tendency of being conditioned so this is the problem of being human. We have a perceptual operative called the brain, which stores memory. When this memory interferes with our seeing things with our perception, then indeed the vast response influences our present response. To be creative is a challenge in the sense that we have to transcend that immediacy, that urgency of seeing. Without that urgency the mind has the tendency of succumbing to the brain's memories and only sees through the brain's memory. Creativity in other words is not easy; it requires a process that includes preparation and some unconscious processing, and then creative insight and discontinuous parts come to us. Ordinarily thoughts will just be parts of memory.

If we want to change our life today so that it is different tomorrow, can we do that?

Yes we can, but it requires creativity. It requires the ability to respond without sifting through past memories. It requires cohesiveness of intention. It requires purposefulness. We have to really wake up to the fact that we are not random human beings responding to chance events in the world. We are actually a purposeful consciousness. The universe has a purpose; it evolves in order to make better and better representation of things we call love, beauty, justice, truth, goodness—those things Plato called archetypes. When we wake up to this purposefulness, we get a focus. Without tuning to the purposefulness of the universe it all seems meaningless and then we become hedonistic and involved in looking at things that are pleasurable and avoiding things that are painful.

Ordinary dreams like the so-called American Dream—obtaining a big house or an expensive car—seem to satisfy us. The

American Dream is really the pursuit of happiness. We forget that it is the pursuit of life, liberty, and happiness that we seek. Liberty ultimately includes creative freedom. Without creative freedom, liberty means nothing. Liberty is just liberty to take the flavor of ice cream that you like. That is the very application of liberty. We have lost touch with the necessity of creative freedom. Today we have crises on our hands so we need innovation and creativity to get us out of these crises, so people are talking about creativity again. What we need is to not only talk about creativity, but talk about an entire paradigm shift. We have got to get out of this very myopic materialist worldview.

People often say to me, "How does one wake up to that? Tell me what button to push."

I wish it could just be a button to push; that would be simple, wouldn't it? Button-pushing works only with material machines. We are human beings and our creativity is latent only because we succumb to our conditioning. To get out of our conditioning we have to go to an entirely different practice. It requires preparation, waiting for things to gel in the unconscious, which we call unconscious processing. Only then comes insight. Even when we get a discontinuous insight, a thought that has never occurred before, even then we have to manifest that insight into a product. That product could be ourselves, which of course is a tremendous accomplishment of transformation in the very way we start out things in the world, our perspective changes. This kind of thing is not easy, but on the other hand it is not difficult either.

Have you met resistance from the physics community about this?

Well of course. But, you know, the resistance is still fairly benign. The materialists mainly do not engage with these aspects of physics. In other words, they try to take the high road approach so far. Although there are some signs that they are slightly engaging.

How do they deal with the random event generator of Dean Radin?

The random event generator of course supports the quantum view. Dean Radin had an idea that if random number generators usually measure chance whether something is to chance, a chance event, a materialist event, a random event, or if something has consciousness built into it in terms of intention. Quantum physics says that consciousness chooses, and choice—as Gregory Bateson said a long time ago—is the opposite of randomness. Radin thought that random number generators used in a place where lots of people are playing would generate numbers that deviate maximally from randomness. And he verified this idea while working in very interesting situations including people in a football field, when a game is on. In those situations, Radin found that the intention of people *would* cause deviation from randomness. Whereas in other situations where people are scatterbrained and they are not particularly intending anything the random number generator would behave normally.

How does physics address that?

It's very simple. Today, science is very segmented. So, which branch of science would you think this particular data corresponds to? If you said psychology, think again. Psychology has become a completely behavioristic and cognitive science as far as academia is concerned. Biology? No. This has nothing to do with biological beings. Physics, definitely not. Only quantum physicists like me would be delighted with such an experiment. But who in physics worries about consciousness and intention except a few of us who are interested in the interpretation of quantum physics. So in this way, the scientists can go ahead talking about such things. So Radin gets the label of being a parapsychologist. And you know, parapsychology is a very restricted, small field to which materialists' attention is mainly in terms of degrading it. You know, there are debunking magazines and journals that materialists publish regularly to discredit parapsychology. Other than that, mainstream science hardly pays any attention.

So, if consciousness can indeed influence events, as it's been demonstrated to do, then it has to be true that consciousness can form peace in the world.

Yes. Of course it has to be true. And therefore, the new physical principles that we are introducing—that consciousness does choose out of quantum possibilities the actual event that we experience—is extremely important to bring to the attention of the public.

Let's talk about health and levels of awareness. Would you agree that we have at least three levels of awareness: sensate, cognitive, and self? What role does being conscious play regarding your health and the manifestation of disease or sickness? Are you sick because your organ is sick or are you sick because there is downward causation?

Your questions are so wonderfully pertinent to the dilemmas of life. Again, the problem with materialist science is that allopathy—the culture of the physical body—is the only treatment we have. Allopathy is also called modern medicine. Every form of medicine that is being used is called modern medicine, so I don't like that phrase; I prefer allopathy. Allopathy is based on the idea that the physical body is the only thing we have. All illness must be because of illness of an organ.

This is a fallacy not only of concept, but also a fallacy of what we actually see. There are now diseases like chronic fatigue where you test all the organs and they are all Okay. There's nothing wrong with any of the organs and yet the person is constantly complaining of pain. Where does the pain come from? Empirically and experimentally this kind of attitude that the physical body is the only place where disease can come is wrong. It is just incomplete.

What other bodies do we have? In the new science and also in old traditions, they were not so tied up with the materialist prejudices that we have today in our science. In the new science, consciousness has four compartments of possibility; four kinds of experiences that are very easy to see. We have sensate; we sense the physical. We have feelings; what do we feel? We feel vital energies of the vital world, so that is another world of possibilities. Then we think; we have mental facility and that comes somewhat from participating in a mental world. Finally we even have an archetypal world, a world of value that gives us intuition. That is a world that is so subtle that we can only intuit it. So, four full experiences, all different worlds. Consciousness is a multi-verse.

In this view, we have a body in each of these worlds: we have a physical body, a vital body, a mental body, and intuitive body. Any of these bodies can become diseased. Any of these bodies may not be working properly or we are not accessing it properly. We are not moving it properly or we are not using it properly. We have alternative systems of medicine which believe that when these bodies are not right, disease can come. Unless you remove the defect of these more *subtle* bodies, you are not going to remove the symptoms permanently; they will come back.

This is where allopathic medicine is completely helpless and hopeless. They only respond to symptoms. The symptoms come back and again you have to take medicine. These allopathic medicines are very harmful to our bodies, actually. They are poisons and they eventually get us into serious problems in other parts of the physical body. In the name of healing we are using killing medicines, literally. The real answer to chronic disease is to go to vital body medicine. Go to mind-body medicine where mind and the vital bodies will be treated to bring balance into synchrony with the physical, and pain will go away.

Let's talk about these alternative medicines: frequency medicine, electromagnetic frequency machines.

Well, I would rather call them the new science we have introduced as the four bodies: physical, vital, mental, and supra-mental bodies. I would rather call this medicine or system vital body medicine, mind-body medicine, something like that, instead of vibrational medicine or frequency medicine. Those names were used when we did not have a very clear picture. I've written a book called *The Quantum Doctor* where the picture is completely clarified between all alternative medicine practices and their relationship with conventional allopathic medicine. So now that we have a good theory there is no need to use such very ambiguous notations as vibrational medicine or frequency medicine.

So, vital body medicine and those traditional medicines like acupuncture; Ayurvedic medicine, which uses herbs; mind-body medicine, which I've already mentioned; homeopathy, and chakra medicine are all vital body medicines. All of these medicines treat the etheric bodies. That is another name for the vital bodies they are sometimes called etheric bodies.

What is your definition of mind?

Mind. This is a very important question! Mind, following Descartes in the west, has been interpreted in a very general way; too general. It includes consciousness. It also includes what we normally call mentation—mind in terms of thinking. So, because thinking and thinker both are included in the word mind, it has caused enormous confusion. So, when I'm talking about consciousness, I mean the consciousness that includes the experiencer; the thinker rather than the thinking. Mind is the place where thinking takes place. So, mind, more explicitly, is the compartment of consciousness, with whose help consciousness settles on the meaning aspect of the world. Mind helps consciousness to give meaning to the physical and other beings of consciousness, other states of consciousness. Mind is the meaning giver, so to speak.

I assume that you don't believe the mind is contained within the brain.

No.

Do you think the mind is contained within our electromagnetic field, within our aura as some metaphysics . . .

No. Mind is completely different from anything material. As I said, mind is the domain of meaning. Recently, Roger Penrose, the great English mathematician, has proven mathematically that computers cannot process meaning. In other words, meaning is outside the purview of the material world. It does not belong to the material world so there has to be a world where the objects are objects of meaning. And this is the world that I call the mind. This is the world that traditionally we have called the mind until Descartes changed it when he included mind and consciousness together. Everything internal became mind in Descartes' term. That has caused enormous confusion in the west.

That's one of the problems I'm hoping to gain insight on with this project. The norm of the population walking around in the world is under the impression that the brain is the thinking mechanism. Personally, I don't believe that to be true. I believe that the brain is the processor of the thinking mechanism. What are your thoughts on that?

Well, we are talking about very subtle language here. I sympathize with what you are trying to say. Can I make it more accurate so that it will be more scientifically accurate? What we say is that the mind is the meaning-giver. Brain makes it a presentation of mental meaning. Once the brain has presented a mental meaning, then certainly it is possible to say that the brain can process meaning because brain can process meaning which has already been presented in the brain. So it's like the brain has mental software. And we use this brain's mental software, namely our past memory, in our thinking. We don't always process new meaning, which would require going outside of what we have memorized, what we remember to our brain. In that sense, a slight confusion can occur. And materialists, of course, take advantage of this confusion. They identify brain as mind. But in that, they also negate creativity completely. What is the proof that materialists are wrong? The proof is that creativity is a very well established experience that we have. With creativity we certainly can change the world—to serve the universe, as Freeman Dyson once said. Therefore, this has causal efficacy. Creativity has causal efficacy, no question about it. That proves that brain cannot possibly be mind because mind has creative meaning in addition to conditioned meaning that brain has already made representations of.

What do you believe to be the source of creativity and intentionality?

The source is consciousness itself . . . the subject that we become in a creative experience. The subject, that creative self, which sometimes we call by a very holy name, like the Holy Spirit—the spirit or the spiritual in us—is that which is the source to which the creativity becomes apparent. The insight comes, and the insight comes in the form of new meaning.

Personally, I'm happy to hear a scientist admit that.

Well, it is about time. Science has not been pursuing the main job of being a human, which is to pursue, to discover, the soul. We have been ignoring the soul. We have even been ignoring *meaning*, it turns out. We have been talking about the mind, but because we talk about mind synonymously with the brain we have become extremely narrow in our attitudes—in our *living*. What we do today in our society has become so mundane. Day by day it becomes more mundane. Why? We become so sold on these identities that scientists sell us—practically brainwashed—that that we forget about the new, completely. We just go on repeating the same experiences. We even bring up our children to do that.

That's right—conditioning. And I believe it is the job of the scientific community to bring this to the forefront because people are taught from the very beginning in kindergarten that science is the ultimate truth and spirituality is a fairy tale. And this won't change until science tells the masses that there's something more to this than merely the brain, they're not going to listen . . . because that's who they've been conditioned to listen to.

Yes. So it is imperative to recognize the paradigm shift that is taking place within science. However, at the same time, remember, all of us ultimately *are* that consciousness, the whole that I call quantum consciousness, which traditions have called God. We have in potentia that same potency as the God consciousness. Therefore, although temporarily, we may be taken over in one culture or another culture by aberrations, by limitations, by conditioning . . . it is definitely not the permanent state that we are going to be stuck in. It has happened many times. That phenomenon itself is a spectacular aberration. But we say, well, that is the consciousness that is going to be identified as the human consciousness so human consciousness is not this corrupted climate of today. It is far beyond that and it is just a temporary disease. Materialism is like a disease in our midst and it has to be healed. It has to be healed. The new paradigm of science is part of it. You are part of it by having the tenacity to get funds for the kind of radio show that you are doing now. So, you know, we are all playing the role of healing this. And the healing will take place. It is taking place.

Let's refer back to the random event generator for a minute. If it's true—and I believe it is, because I believe in Dean Radin's work—that consciousness can affect how the balls drop in that machine, then it has to be true that if people would understand that they are the source of creativity and intention, or the oneness, or the God source, or God consciousness . . . that if they put out thoughts of agape or positive intent for their fellow mankind, something positive has to happen.

Yes, but it is important for us to recognize why our intentions fall short; why they become so narrow in terms of their potentiality. The reason is that we do not work on ourselves to transform into that bigger consciousness. We become limited. In a limited consciousness, even when we are thinking of agape, it is just thinking. We are not *feeling* our heart to be expanded . . . we are not feeling the energy in the heart. We are not even feeling an expansive feeling in the region of the heart in the body.

Most people have forgotten what mystics refer to as the *journey to the heart*, especially in the technological part of the world; especially in the west. We suppress emotions, and by suppressing emotions we lose touch with a very easy way of expanding our consciousness, namely, coming down from the head; bringing the energy into the heart. In my workshops, I teach people how to bring the energy down to the heart when talking to other people. When you learn to do that, then agape—unconditional love—comes to us in a very natural way. And we know this because we feel the heart to be expanded. We feel warm in the heart.

So with that kind of signature, then if we intend, the intention has a much better potency, a much better chance of coming true. Then when we intend world peace, then it has much more of an affect than if we just do it in a thinking way. Because when we are thinking we are already narrow. Actually because I am so much in my head, when my energy goes to the third chakra, the navel (one's personal power center), I become proud or I become egotistic, or I create conflict. This is why world peace does not come about because we try to do it piecemeal. We try to do it by trying to change others but not ourselves. We have to do both. We have to try to change others, of course. But, we have to also have to try to change ourselves.

I can't say anything but yes. I'm of the opinion in some of the work that I'm doing, that anytime you think a thought it's going to cause neurotransmitters to fire, and something happens. And I believe that when you go to the position of your heart, with love in your heart, and not just in your brain, in your mind that it causes something to happen, neurotransmitters, hormones and other chemicals to be released into your body that causes your heart to be filled with blood, and it feels good. I think that it also changes your resonant field. And if it's true that this entire world is made up of atoms, then there can't be any disconnection. So, if your resonant field changes to a more positive resonance then it can't help but affect the resonant frequency of the entire world. The affect may be subtle, but it's still an influence. Does that make any sense to you?

In quantum physics it happens because of a phenomenon we call quantum non-locality. People can get correlated. And what is so amazing is that human beings are already quite capable of correlating with one another because we share the same consciousness. Consciousness is the ground of all being. We all come from that one consciousness. There is now laboratory proof that one consciousness is real. In other words, although in our ordinary state of the ego we don't experience it, we can in many circumstances experience this one consciousness that we are one with others because we are connected in consciousness. There is a nonlocal consciousness, without any signals, a signal-less connection that we share. With that we can influence people, even without the intermediary of electromagnetic waves.

Would that be the research that's been done on the double slits with the electrons?

Well, that's part of it. That's part of the same research. The double-slit experiment provides great proof that there is indeed non-locality.

What do you mean by the ground of all being? Do you mean God, or whatever someone might call that entity?

Well, technicalities aside, yes, that is what I mean. Most traditions prefer to use the word God in that sense; God is the *creative agent of this ground of being.* The ground of being, philosophically speaking, has been thought of as eternal. Anything that is eternal and non-changing is outside of space and time. Nothing can happen. For creativity to come into the picture, for things to happen, we need some limitation so God is not exactly the entire ground of being but God is the creative agent of the ground of being after some limitations have been established.

So what is ground of being if it is more than God?

Ground of being is sometimes called the godhead. It is eternity that is always there in the background. Sometimes people ask me when I teach Big Bang Theory what is before the Big Bang? Good question! The only answer is that before the Big Bang is eternity, which is always present. So, "consciousness is the ground of being" is a good answer to that perpetual question, otherwise it could project infinitely—what is before, what is *before?* With eternity, the buck stops there because nothing *can* be before. It has no past, no present, and no future. Eternity contains all possibilities—everything that will be. Everything is included—there is no time in it. To get time into the picture, to get creativity into the picture, to get creation of the universe into the picture, we must have limitations, such as we must have some laws of the universe. We must bring in meaning; we must bring in the idea that there are definite templates of biological being to work with. After all of these limitations comes the creation of matter. Matter has to then make representations of what went before it. Representation of mental meaning, representation of blueprints of biological functions, etc.

Do you have a theory of how the original observer came to be?

Yes. The original observer is the one-celled creature from which we have all evolved. Some 4.5 billion years ago that took place. That was a monumental event. Before then everything was just possibilities. Of course we cannot rule out that there are other planets where other such one-celled creatures have arisen. Within that caveat I can say that, indeed, before life appeared on the scene, everything was just quantum possibilities for consciousness to choose from. But there was no manifest consciousness or manifest observer and therefore no choice and therefore it just remained *possible* things. We had a possible universe so to speak, but no actuality. That moment of creation of what John Wheeler calls "the completion of the meaning circuit," completion of the life circuit, the whole universe was created—the Big Bang included—going backwards in time.

I don't quite understand going backwards in time.

Well, you have to think. It is intriguing but it is true. Life came about 4.5 billion years ago. The Big Bang, our latest calculations are showing, probably happened 13.5 billion years ago. This creates a problem because at the Big Bang, with that heat, life could never exist, so this is the way it has to be. It must be that when consciousness chooses, then everything manifests . . . even if it is a delayed choice. Although the first living cell chose 4.5 billion years ago, all the things that went before that—like planets with atmosphere, solar systems, galaxies, and the Big Bang itself—have to be there in the whole causal lineage. The entire causal lineage manifests right at that moment but the entire space and time is created with it. Time itself was created in that chronological way that logic says it has to happen. Our choice now precipitates the actuality from possibilities, then, going backwards in time.

Did things evolve, or did things spontaneously appear, or a combination of both?

This is a very, very good question. For a long time spiritual traditions and religions thought that there is no evolution because God creates. Initially it didn't make sense to people, I suppose, that God cannot create instantly. This is the mistake we made in those days because we didn't realize that the universe is lawful. Many things in the universe look so accidental, so full of chance happenings, we did not fathom that there could be laws of the universe; that God works within laws. When science was established we found laws so natural scientists were very much interested in what the laws set out, even for manifestation. There is no longer any need to assume that arbitrary things can happen. Naturally the idea in Genesis that God created the world all at once—although I know there is a metaphorical interpretation how we can avoid that particular meaning—but still, mainly people interpreted it as saying that God created everything at once. The scientific evidence collected shows clearly in the fossil records that evolution exists. There are simple fossils initially, then single cell and multiple celled animals, and then invertebrates, vertebrates, and all that.

The theory that Darwin gave has some big gaps, called fossil gaps. The fossils, according to Darwin's Theory, should have been continuously laid out. They are not continuous. There are gaps in them. What do the gaps mean? This is where I have developed a new theory based on the worldview of what quantum physicists are giving us, and that consciousness is the ground of being. In this view, you don't have to assume that evolution arose from continuous mechanisms; chance mutations and natural selection from the mutation. We don't have to assume that. Instead what we say is, yes, there is evolution, but the evolution is an evolution of consciousness. When looked at from the consciousness point of view, creativity is always there. There is conditioned action, but there is also creative action. When we become conditioned, things become continuous. Have you noticed our stream of consciousness is quite continuous? But it is creativity that is intermittently taking place and that is what enables us to start new phases of life. For example, almost everyone is aware today of midlife transition. We change very quickly during certain periods. Biological evolution is the same way. There are some quick instantaneous changes that take place, and that is what explains the fossil gaps.

How does the information in intention come from the ground of all being into materialism? How does it get there? Is it signaling?

What is the driving force? You are asking a very intelligent question. What is the driving purpose of the universe? We just talked about creativity and evolution; I've written a book on it: *Creative Evolution*. Why go through all of that? What not stay in the unmanifest? In fact, this is a problem for some people. Many people think that God is perfect therefore the world should be perfect, but here is the catch: evolution gives us the way out. Evolution says that evolution takes place in such a way that, initially, beings are not so perfect. The idea of evolution is that we begin as imperfect beings, but we try to become perfect. Why does God manifest? Why not stay in perfection forever? Because in the unmanifest—in eternity—nothing happens. Why do things happen? Things happen because we want to get to that perfection eventually, but in manifestation. We say that there are these archetypes of value— love, beauty, justice, truth, and goodness being the five major archetypes we recognize. Can we be loving by just wishing it? Can we *be* just by just wishing? No; we have to struggle for it. We have to evolve toward it. The idea of evolution is that, initially, we are not very loving. Initially we are not very perfect. Eventually we evolve towards being loving beings; we evolve towards perfection. We evolve towards justice, towards goodness. You can see that we evolved. In the last century itself major events took place that took us to a more just society.

Of course now we have a backlash. We made progress like the proverbial monkey going up the bamboo pole. You go up one foot and fall three feet. The taste of that "just society" remains with us and eventually we catch up again, and when we catch up we go a little bit further. We fall three feet but then we'll climb four feet so it will be a net gain and that's the way we have always proceeded.

I would like you to explain delayed choice and anthropic principle.

Anthropic principle is a good example of delayed choice. Without delayed choice the anthropic principle would be unexplained. The world does go towards establishing consciousness. With anthropic principle, the world is designed in such a way that eventually consciousness will come about. In quantum physics we need consciousness to have a manifest world, so how does the world manifest? Only when consciousness comes about does the world manifest, when the circle is complete. The world needs consciousness to manifest and consciousness needs the conditions to be right so that consciousness can manifest. This circularity is the circularity behind the anthropic principles. We need the universe; the universe needs us. The universe cannot manifest without the observer. The observer cannot manifest without the universe and its evolution.

How does this correlate with free will?

Free will is that ultimate causation that is beyond all material causation; the causation that we started in this dialogue. Remember when I said that quantum physics is the physics of possibilities and consciousness is needed to choose from these possibilities? That choice, when made freely without past conditioning, is what we call free will. We do have free will but it is at a higher state of consciousness. It is at that consciousness that we call God. I call it quantum consciousness.

The average individual walking around is not conscious.

Most are not particularly conscious because we are not really using the freedom of choice to engage real consciousness. In other words, we lead sort of a zombie-like existence where we are more or less conditioned beings; more or less machines. The trick is to

choose to be *more* or *less*. We *can* be more; it is within our preroga-
tive. For example, we can start saying no to conditioning.

*Yes. So, if someone says to me, "Yes, I have free will—I can go
swimming today, or I can go to the grocery store" . . . is that free will?*

No, that is not free will. We don't require will to explain that.
Materialist scientists have very good models of neural nets in their
model, the brain, and the neural nets are conditioned to move in
various pathways. One pathway is for you to go to swimming, and
one pathway is for you to go to the ice cream parlor instead. Both
will satisfy your desire to avoid heat. Ice cream is good, but it makes
you fat, so swimming is better; it makes you trim. But sometimes
we do this or do that according to our history of conditioning.
That's the materialist model. It works. We don't need creativity of
consciousness to choose between swimming and ice cream, right?

*What are your thoughts on the manifestation of intent into physi-
cal reality? What I mean by that is, the average people walking on the
street don't believe that intent is powerful and they say, well if I could
manifest whatever it is that I intend, then why can't I manifest the
Rolls-Royce that I've been wanting?*

Yes. In the '70s, there was an organization which used to teach
how to manifest Rolls-Royces and when you failed to manifest a
Rolls-Royce, they promptly went to the manifestation of parking
spaces in busy downtown areas.

Kidding aside, it's the same problem—the ego—the narrow-
ness of consciousness that keeps us from manifesting our intention.
When we fail, we identify our limitation as the limitation of intention. Intention has the potency of god consciousness. But we have
to intend in the right frame of consciousness. If we are in the nar-
rowness of the ego, then already our intention is not going to have
any effect on the cosmic consciousness, where such manifestations
are open as a possibility.

But if we are wide enough, for example, in the heart consciousness that we just talked about, we become somewhat more
expanded, so our chances become better. If we then arrive at

mystical states of consciousness, such as Jesus, Buddha, and others talked about, then we become really synonymous with cosmic consciousness. Then our chance of manifesting things becomes even better. So it depends on how wide in consciousness we want to be. How much expansion can we attain? Because in those expanded states, what happens that scares some people is that we don't *want* any fancy car; we only want good for everyone. We don't want any individual gratification of the material kind. Our selfishness goes away. So people become afraid of it. When they think about expanded consciousness, they don't want it. They only want their selfish goodies and satisfaction of their senses.

So, we have some growing up to do. We are still children in terms of maturity of consciousness.

I agree. Do you think it would matter how focused your intent is? For example, I believe that intent can be somewhat like a puzzle. Say you want to manifest a Rolls-Royce in your front yard. You've got to put out the intent of the longitude and the latitude and how you want that to come. Otherwise, the Rolls-Royce might come in scattered pieces . . . and you'd have to go gather those pieces and put them together.

Very good point! That is one reason that intentions in those expanded states of consciousness really do not involve such trivia as a Rolls-Royce. But again, we really have to learn the subtleties and the enormity of the potential we are in. We have not even begun to endeavor into mental creativity . . . into discovery of new meanings. I mean a few of us—the great artists, the great scientists, and the great philosophers—do it. But the rest of us are quite satisfied to just experience a very narrow range of mental meaning. So, to come to a place where you can play creatively in the physical domain, like manifesting something that did not exist in the material domain before . . . that's a huge order. To even ponder it, to even think about it, blows your mind. Because you recognize that you're literally going against the grain of materialist physics, creating new material out of nothing. So, it's that kind of creativity, and we think about doing that whereas we have not even explored a much simpler kind of creativity which is creativity of mental meaning. So, we have a long way to go. That does not mean we become stymied. As the Chinese proverb says, a ten-thousand-mile journey begins with the first step. So, we have to learn to be creative. Mentally creative first, then creative with our vital energy—energies of love—and then finally creative at the material level.

What made me start thinking about the focused intent was a story I heard about a man obsessed with a blue Silver Cloud Rolls Royce. He looked in the newspaper every Sunday at all the ones that were for sale, looked in the car magazines . . . and one day he saw one for sale for $50. He just couldn't believe it. He called this woman to ask if she was serious about selling this fabulous car for $50. And she said yes. So he rushed over, thinking maybe it didn't have an engine in it. And it was in perfect shape. He took the paperwork to his lawyer, and the lawyer said it's all in order. When the deal was closed, he asked, "Why did you sell that car for $50? You could sell it for $50,000." And she said, "Well, my husband left me for his secretary, and they moved down to our place in Palm Springs. The divorce settlement was fair; I'm taken care of. He told me that the only thing he wanted me to do was to sell his car and send him the check."

So, the point is the guy got his Rolls-Royce. He manifested a Rolls-Royce. But what he forgot to do was to manifest the money to take care of it. So he can't drive it, because he can't afford the tags, the insurance, or the maintenance. But he has his Rolls-Royce. He forgot to manifest with clean intent.

Yes, this is a good example of how intentions can work even at the mental level to help at the physical level. Sometimes, when we intend, the power of intention also has a power to open us up to some extent. So, you know, if you want to use this man's intention as an example of how this man manifested, I don't want to object too much. You know, because we all routinely go outside of our ego occasionally.

What would your perspective on karma be regarding this? Let's take somebody that's in a poverty situation . . . someone who's living in a poverty state, in filth. And they sit all the time, and they intend and intend and intend that they're going to have money, that that money doesn't come. Do you think that karma, assuming karma is real, has anything to do with why it doesn't come? In other words, do you think that you are placed in this life for the god-consciousness to experience certain experiences in this physical body, in this hologram? And that no matter what we do that is the intent of this life in this body for the things that don't happen. I mean it's just what is.

Karma is nothing but conditioning from past lives. Any kind of conditioning keeps us from becoming expanded in consciousness. Conditioning is what produces the ego identity. Ego identity is nothing but a confluence of all of our conditioned habit patterns. So, karma is just a big part of it, and indeed it keeps us from manifesting intention. But karma is not compulsory. Conditioning is not compulsory. We can, in spite of karma and conditioning, be creative and we can therefore expand our consciousness and overcome barriers to our intentions from coming true.

We can do it, but we have to know about creativity. We have to engage in the creative process, which has its own findings, and is a very rich literature today. People can get a lot of hints about how to be creative today that didn't exist even fifty years ago. So, if somebody is stuck in karma and conditioning, I say to them wake up, help is available. Use some of that help that we are offering. This is the new technology of the new paradigm of science. We don't have flashy things like materialist science does, but consciousness science is producing its own technology which can be very powerful and is very rewarding in terms of satisfaction.

You just made a reference to reincarnation. Do you believe that we literally die, get put in the ground, and come back in another body? Or do you believe we all exist simultaneously all at one time?

It depends on what language you feel comfortable with. We say we get buried and then we come back in another body that paints a certain picture that's subject to a lot of misinterpretation. The essence that we call our soul consists of habit patterns—mental and vital—plus the *supramental*, being some of the godliness that we also carry as potential within us all, that continues on after our death. So, these continued patterns we can experience in a future time. This is a valid interpretation of what happens in the incarnation, and data actually supports it.

What we normally call the soul isn't anything of a material substance; it's not substantial. Instead, it's a pattern of habits. If somebody in the future uses or inherits these patterns, that person can legitimately be called my reincarnation, but not in the sense of a soul traveling from my body into that body or another future body. Transmigration is more subtle than that, and that subtlety has to be understood. So, the answer to your question is yes and no. It depends. How far do you want to go in your understanding? If you want to do it completely, it can be done. I have shown in the book, *Physics of the Soul* that a complete understanding today is within reach. It has been achieved. Science can understand reincarnation completely. The data is there to verify this understanding. So at that level, one can. On the other hand, if you want a quicker level, there's danger you'll misinterpret or misunderstand some of the steps. Still, essentially, you cannot misunderstand too much, so long as you recognize that the physical body is gone. The way we carry on some of our rituals is very misleading because we think that there is still something in the buried body. Those things are just tremendously misleading. The physical body is dead. It's finished. But the more subtle aspects of ourselves, namely our vital, mental, supramental—our consciousness itself—those things live on. In particular the patterns of those things that we collected in our life, those patterns live on in a very real sense. And they can be recycled. And that recycling of these patterns is what we call reincarnation.

Do you believe that the consciousness is contained within the soul? And if you say yes to that question, do you believe that that consciousness' soul would be contained within a frequency or a field? How would it be contained? How would it exist? It has to exist some way.

This is an interesting question because you are using "frequency," which refers to wave, which suggests that this intuitive language started emerging a little bit before this quantum theory developed. So if the language is changed just a bit, it will approach the very essential truth of what you are saying. In other words, don't take "frequency" literally. But take the idea that it's a waveness. Waveness means a potentia. It's a wave in potentiality, that's what quantum possibility waves are. So, getting back to the essence I was talking about . . . these patterns are changes in quantum potentia; changes in quantum possibility waves. So they're sort of like frequency modulation, like an FM radio. These are frequency modulations. Not the frequency itself; modulation *of* frequency. So what happens is that we have similar modulation of these waves of possibility. In other words, the probabilities of these possibilities are modulated by how we experience our life. How we condition ourselves, how we develop our patterns.

So in that sense it is very much like frequency modulated waves going from one region to another, but not *exactly* like that. This has to be understood not in terms of a substance like a wave actually traveling a little distance as a signal, but rather, as just some patterns of potential being transferred from one place to another.

How does the brain interpret the messages that consciousness is delivering?

It's a little bit subtle. Let me give you the actual quantum model of how this transmission takes place from one brain to another. Instead of thinking that one brain is emitting some electromagnetic wave which is modulated, and another brain is then receiving it, for which indeed there is no evidence . . . and that's the materialist argument. They immediately say, well, this we can disprove. But the problem is that we cannot rule out the phenomenon. Because telepathy takes place even though it can be disproved due to electromagnetic waves just by simply putting the psychics in electromagnetically impervious chambers. We have done that, and telepathy still exists. So somehow the information is going from one brain to another although it is not going with the help of electromagnetic waves. So how does it go, then?

In the consciousness model, it's more subtle. We say the potentia is present in the cosmic consciousness—which is one for the two observers; the two telepaths. So the communication occurs how? One observer is thinking something, namely choosing something from the meaning domain, and the other observer, because she is correlated with the first observer, is choosing something of identical or almost identical meaning from the spectrum of possibilities that she is experiencing in her mind. And so that particular brain makes a representation of that mental meaning, which then is correlated with that mental meaning, which then is correlated with the first observer's mental meaning and the first observer's brain. This is why in the new experiments we find that brain potential from one brain to another can be transferred without electromagnetic signals. This is the newest of experiments and this is revolutionizing our attitude toward non-local consciousness. Because if brain potential electric activity in one brain can be transferred to another brain without an electrical connection, without an electromagnetic wave, then how can you deny there is a subtle, non-local connection between the two brains? And it is this connection that we call consciousness.

What is your position on free will? Do you believe it exists? For example, I can say that I'm going to the grocery store tomorrow at three o'clock. You know, that's my free will to choose that I decided to go to the grocery store. But, in actuality, I have absolutely no way of guaranteeing that even though I fully intend being there at three o'clock, source or the God-consciousness, whoever it is, may not see that fit for me. I may be stuck in traffic, I may have an accident, I may get a phone call that keeps me detained. My kids may start acting up. So in actuality, at the source of consciousness do you believe that free will exists to do whatever we choose? If so, why can't I guarantee that I'll be at the grocery store at three o'clock?

I do not know if you could ever guarantee that, because it depends also on other factors which of course are dependent on how other people are exerting their free—or not so free—will. Actually in my opinion, the phrase free will can be used in two ways. And you are using it one way now, which is, the free will of choosing between conditioned alternatives. In other words, you have the conditioning of being able to elect transport and you have the will to go to a grocery store and you have access to it at any time. So you have a certain conditioning that you can go to grocery stores whenever they are open. And depending on the conditioning you are choosing this particular date, this particular time to go there. So it's a free will of choosing something that the brain already knows you have done, you have memory, you are choosing this particular date and time to do it. One kind of free will. But this is not totally free, because it depends on conditioned learning that you have already accomplished. There's nothing totally free about it.

If you are giving a lecture to an audience, what are some examples of truly free will that they can understand?

One of my favorite examples is when you agonize over an ethical decision. Think about when you agonize over an ethical matter. Sometimes ethical decisions are very tricky; they require so much finesse, and choice becomes an agony because ethical point is not unambiguous. I often have this debate with well-meaning people because sometimes I like making radical statements. For example, I made a statement at a lecture saying that all conscious people don't believe in truth telling in a trivial way. People got very upset stating are you suggesting that people should lie if they become conscious? They have never encountered the ethical dilemma of choice that we sometimes face.

Let's say you see somebody running, and in the next moment you see someone following that person running, and the person following has a gun. It doesn't take a genius to see that if this person asks you if you saw a person running, you don't immediately tell the person oh yes, he went that way. Instead you hesitate and say something that is neutral or misleading because you don't want anyone to be shot to death. But if you realize this person with a gun is a police officer, then you might again change your mind, but that moment is a moment of creativity; the moment of your choice. You didn't succumb to your conditioning immediately, that if a person asks you something in an authoritative voice, then you immediately obey. You didn't do that; you didn't succumb to the conditioned action. Instead you held on, thinking ok, wait a minute . . . and that's the opening for a creative decision. So in this kind of situation it is pretty easy to see that we have causal efficacy and we have to bring it into manifestation, and we do. Most people are able to recognize in that case that yes we may have to tell a lie to save a person's life.

In its essence, free will is about creativity. When we are creative, then we are exercising freedom because we are choosing something that we didn't know before. I am choosing something that is totally new. So freedom is that which cannot be predicted, that was not experienced before, that is totally new, that we have no control over. You see what I'm getting at?

So the first kind of freedom is important—the freedom to be able to choose from among one's own conditioned prerogatives— and we fight for it. When our forefathers said give me liberty or give me death, they were talking about that kind of freedom. It is important, but it is not the ultimate freedom in the sense of creative freedom. It is not freedom to create something that is completely new.

I guess I think that we're not actually driving this car known as the physical body. I feel like we are toddlers sitting in the back seat, strapped into a little car seat with a little yellow steering wheel, and we think we are driving that car.

We think that we are driving. Exactly! And when we take on that creativity, then we are really driving. And to tell you the truth, the human body/mind is not ready to drive that way all the time. Even beings like Jesus and Buddha were not in their holy spirit world all the time; only some of the time.

And when they are, they speak in parables. They speak in words, in languages that we don't understand. They say things that are outrageous, like "I am God, I am the truth," and this causes tremendous confusion because we ordinary humans think, how can they be like that? How can they say things like that? And so we crucify them.

Dr. Goswami, is there anything that you would like to make known before we end?

I would certainly encourage everyone to undertake this grand consciousness research that is personally open to every one of us. It does not require much of laboratory. It does not require expensive instrumentation. It requires a wonderful mind; a creative mind. If we engage creative and loving mind into this consciousness research the world can change and in a very short time!

CHAPTER 5

William Tiller, Ph.D.

William Tiller is a fellow to the American Academy for the Advancement of Science, professor emeritus of Stanford University's Department of Materials Science, spent 34 years in academia after nine years as an advisory physicist with the Westinghouse Research Laboratories. He has published over 250 conventional scientific papers, and several patents. In parallel, for over thirty years, he has been avocationally pursuing serious experimental and theoretical study of the field of psychoenergetics which will very likely become an integral part of "tomorrow's" physics. In this new area, he has published an additional 100 scientific papers and *The Science of Crystallization: Macroscopic Phenomena, Defect Generation, The Science of Crystallization: Microscopic Interfacial Phenomena, Psychoenergetic Science: A Second Copernican-Scale Revolution, Some Science Adventures with Real Magic, Conscious Acts of Creation: The Emergence of a New Physics, Science and Human Transformation: Subtle Energies, Intentionality and Consciousness.*

Eva: Welcome, Dr. Bill Tiller. I'm looking forward to discussing your book, Psychoenergetics, but before we get into that, please give us a brief summary of your professional background . . . which is in engineering, correct?

Bill: Well, engineering and physics. So I think of myself as a physicist with a bent towards applications, and as a physicist I've been working in the area of materials for a long, long time. Another term would be solid-state physics.

When you began delving into this area of subtle energy research, how did your colleagues respond?

Ha, they thought I was a heretic and wished I was somewhere else. It is unfortunate, but when you step outside the box, people have difficulties. In my own department, I gave up being department chairman in order to have the time outside of my "day-job" to do this kind of work, and most of my department was very unhappy. There were one or two who were okay with it. Most of them thought I had gone off my rocker.

I find it hard to understand why classical science refuses to acknowledge what is as plain as the ink on the paper.

There has been data relative to this kind of work around for a very long time—well over a century—and *good* work too. The difficulty is, it has been an enigma for science since the days of Descartes. The unstated assumption of science for the last 400 years has been that no human qualities of consciousness, intention, emotion, mind, or spirit can significantly impact a well-designed target experiment in physical reality. Those who are in the box unconsciously believe this, so this kind of work is threatening to them because it can't be explained by the conventional paradigm. They would prefer it go away, and put their heads in the sand, thinking it *will* go away, and instead of reading the material, they'll use hubris and words of delusion, and by and large espouse scientism because they have never looked seriously at the data. Truth is always in the data, not in our interpretation of the data.

Perhaps we should clarify at this point that we are not trying to say that classical science is wrong, but that it is unnecessarily limited in its perspective.

Oh, absolutely not. Classical science is very good. Quantum mechanics, as limited as it is, has done great things. But there is nothing in our present quantum mechanics that allows human consciousness to enter the mathematical formulas. The limitation of our present paradigm is that it is all tied to space-time. You cannot use space-time as a reference frame for consciousness. You have to expand the reference frames so that you can begin to see what it means and how it interacts with coarse physical reality.

I started out in Toronto, Canada. I did all my degree work there. Went to work as an advisory physicist at the Westinghouse research labs in Pittsburgh for nine years. I got my wife to leave Canada and come to the U.S. with me. After being at Westinghouse for nine years I then went to Stanford as a full professor, with tenure, fortunately. Back around 1964, my wife and I started daily meditation. Then I became department chair in our department because the man who hired me became ill.

I then went on sabbatical to London—Oxford—during 1970, 71. I got seriously interested in psychoenergetics, as an outgrowth of my daily meditation during the 60s. I read this little book, *Psychic Discoveries Behind the Iron Curtain*, by Ostrander and Schroeder. I knew a great deal about the subject at that time, and yet I was impressed with the scope of the Soviet work. This difficult question kept arising in me, which was, how might this universe be constructed to allow this crazy-seeming stuff to naturally coexist with the traditional physics I was teaching at Stanford every day? And though I had a certain mission to accomplish when I was there for that year, I couldn't get rid of this idea. So I did a project of daily meditation, asking that question.

After six months I had a reasonably well developed answer as to how that might happen. I figured it was really important for someone serious and with a scientific background to work on this. And after thinking about who it might be, I realized it had to be myself. So when I came back to Stanford, I gave up being department chair so I could do this in my spare time. I gave up all my professional committees and all my government committees in order to have enough time to do this in parallel with my traditional science at Stanford. I had to feed my family so I had to keep my day job. So, basically in 1971 I started a second path in my life and have maintained it ever since.

My subtle energy work is essentially divided into thirds: one third is in the experiential development of self—an absolutely essential process for coming to an understanding of this extremely strange stuff. The second third involves continuing the theorizing about the universe and how this other level of reality could interact with our traditional level of reality, and the remaining third is spent designing and conducting experiments to push the envelope and keep the theory honest.

Out of this have come four books, about 150 scientific publications, and twenty-three (free to download from *www.tiller.org*) White Papers plus two DVDs. Anyone interested can learn all about this on my web site, tiller.org. And there we are.

I think the most important reason for getting this information out there is for people to know the power that we all possess as spiritual human beings.

Absolutely! We are much, much more capable than on the average we believe. It's time to recognize the human possibilities of using our consciousness to influence our physical reality; to influence matter, and the properties of matter. All humans have the infrastructure within themselves to do that—and to a very high degree.

Is the bottom line of what you're saying that people can obtain results in physical reality from pure thought?

Certainly pure thought is critically involved. It is a very complicated business and we only know a little bit. The way I look at it is, I like to think of a ladder of understanding with many rungs to it. Over the last 400 years we have worked very hard, very diligently and we've built the first rung . . . the bottom-most rung of this ladder. The work of psychoenergetics is about building the second rung of the ladder, and we've got a long way to go to do it.

We use this word "consciousness" so loosely. What is your definition of consciousness?

I have a personal definition, but I recognize that in general, we don't have an agreed upon definition. I'll tell you mine and I'll tell you what I think we should be doing. My personal definition is that consciousness is a by-product of spirit entering dense matter. Now, that sounds interesting, but most people can't connect to that. Let me write on sort of a mental blackboard the reaction equation of conventional science. We have mass and we have arrows going back and forth to energy. Almost all that we have done in the last 400 years can be effectively put into that metaphor.

Psychoenergetic science expands this premise to mass, with the arrows back and forth to energy, and additional arrows leading back and forth to consciousness. Since we don't all agree what consciousness is—and it will be a while before we do—I would rather say let's not ask what it is; let's ask what it *does*. When we do that, we almost immediately realize that consciousness manipulates information, whether it's a set of numbers to create a sum or divisor or whatever, or it's alphabetical letters that we string together to make words and sentences. If you are a mathematician, it's the stringing together of symbols to make some important equation that interests you, and if you are a jigsaw-puzzle maker, you select strange shapes and put them together to make a map that has a lot of information in it.

Now, we have known for about sixty years that information gained in terms of bits or bit rate can be equated mathematically to a negative entropy change. If there is an increase in information content in a process there is a reduction in entropy. Entropy is really disorder, so it's a reduction of the disorder. It's the building of order. Now, for one-hundred-fifty years, we have known that the thermodynamic driving process is the thermodynamic free energy change in a reaction, and that is comprised of a pressure times volume term plus an internal energy term minus a temperature times the entropy term. So, from the basic fundamentals of thermodynamics, which influence and really drive all processes in nature that we know about in physical reality, entropy is incredibly important.

So now you can see the reaction equation to be mass, with arrows back and forth to energy, and arrows back and forth to information, and arrows back and forth to consciousness. Information is crucial and it connects intimately with internal energy when you think in terms of thermodynamics free energy. I'm sorry that's a bit of a mouthful, but it creates the chain so we can begin to see that our future is going to have to deal with information, our future science. Since information is so crucial when you want to step towards psychoenergetics, you realize that information in living systems can't be described in just space-time. You can't describe the thermodynamic force in terms of just a gradient of a spacial potential function which is the core of our orthodox science in terms of energetics and forces. So you begin to see that you have to expand the reference frame we use to look at nature. Nature is expressing itself in more than distance-time ways.

What I am saying is, all the science that has been done has been very, very good. We have come a long way, but it's only the beginning. It's only the first rung of the ladder and we've got a long, long way to go.

Can you help us understand what all of this means to our everyday lives?

We've found from our experimental data that the human acupuncture meridian/chakra system is at a higher electromagnetic gauge symmetry level than our normal physical reality level. Now, when it's at this higher level, it turns out that the human intention, the human desire, the human effort to have something happen causes a kind of higher dimensional energy to get pumped through this meridian/chakra system, and those energies in turn influence all the other energies of the normal physical reality. We don't know much about this subtle energy factor yet, but it will probably turn out to be what Eastern cultures refer to as Chi.

Our world around us is the coarse electric atom-molecule level of physical reality. If a person works with, focuses on, and disciplines himself to do this "inner work" with a kind of training like muscle-building, then a normal individual becomes an adept. The adept who keeps working becomes a master and the master who keeps working becomes an avatar. We have the infrastructure within ourselves to do things that are called miracles today. What we think of as magic is just some physics outside the conventional paradigm. Humans have the possibility to become incredibly capable beyond their wildest imagination. This stuff is already there. The infrastructure is already there, it just has to be strengthened to be able to handle larger power.

I have a bias of course, like most people. My bias is that we are all spirits having a physical experience as we ride the river of life together. Our spiritual parents dressed us in these bio-body suits and put us in this playpen that we call a universe in order to grow in coherence, develop our gifts of intentionality, and become what we intended to become—co-creators with our spiritual parents. I think that is the path we are on.

In basic terms, are you saying that if we evolve our mind and emotions, that we can actually influence our daily lives in physical reality?

Absolutely! But you have to give it *meaning* in your life. You have to be willing to suspend judgment, go forward, work with it—and see what happens. Be an open-minded individual and learn as much as you can about it and develop yourself inside. Learn meditative techniques. Learn to become inner self-managed and you will find there are other universes within yourself to be explored.

What is the difference between mind and consciousness?

Well, these are things that we have difficulty in discriminating because we don't really know enough. We know that mentation—mental activity—exists, so we know mind exists, driving that activity. In school we learn all kinds of things that require us to use our mind. We know emotions exist; psychologists and psychiatrists work with them all the time. But if you look at physics, you'll see nothing about emotions, intentions, etc., there. My view of experiments that we could talk about are those that we've done and replicated at ten laboratories in the US and Europe. Intention, I think, is at the spirit level of self—which is a higher dimension than the mind level.

Let's define spirit for our readers.

I wish I could. At this stage in our work, I basically define various levels of substance, and there is coarse (or dense) physical matter, with which we are all familiar. You might say that spirit is a much, much, much, much finer level of substance. Or conversely, you can say physical substance is very coarse spirit. But in essence, again, there are rungs of this ladder of understanding, where each rung deals with different levels of substance and within each domain of substance there are many forces. There are many different kinds of energy, just as in our conventional reality or the electric atom/molecule level of reality. Our science has discovered and quantified four fundamental forces: gravity, electromagnetism, the short-range nuclear force, and the long-range nuclear force. It's taken a long time to come to understand those, quantify them, and use them in engineering ways to influence our society.

As we go from the bottom rung up to the next rung, it is reasonable to presume or postulate that we'll find many different kinds of energies and different kinds of substances. We don't have much of a tool base yet to really do that. We've made some discoveries in our laboratory, but it's still just the very beginning. Now, the next level—the third rung—will deal with the domain of emotion, and the fourth rung will deal with the domain of mind. The fifth rung and above will deal with domains of various levels of spirit.

Consciousness is involved everywhere, at all levels. But remember, we are dealing with things that are working hypotheses. We see experimental data that can be interpreted in terms of these things to allow them to make sense. It's currently a provisional view; as we go down the road and we really do good science on these things, we'll learn more and more about them. The dilemma is that all of the funding for scientific research these days, which comes from individual taxes and such, is pretty much all devoted to the bottom rung of the ladder. You don't move this envelope very far forward because you are limited by the financial potential to do the research.

There is definitely a need for funding.

Yes. We are making progress but it is slow. We've done enough to know that we really have something which is quite different than that which my many thesis students did at Stanford working inside the box.

If we had funding, not only would we get more into consciousness and what it avails us in physical reality and our daily lives, but also the thermodynamic free energy potential of the physical vacuum level fields.

Oh yes. These energies that I am talking about will change the face of technology. The stuff we are doing will change everything . . . and enhance every technology that exists in the world today.

People don't believe it but it is there.

It's there. We have some evidence to indicate that it is there. But the degree of it, the magnitude, the shape, the color, the subtle aspects of it . . . we've got a long way to go before we really can master the second rung of the ladder.

I believe that there are gradients in conscious awareness, but some people don't agree, or they just don't get it.

Yes. Let me go back to what I said about my personal definition of consciousness. I'll repeat it. To me, consciousness is a byproduct of spirit entering dense matter. How this looks to me is as follows. If we are active in life and doing things—doing things at physical levels, at emotional levels, at mental levels, and at spiritual levels— in so doing, we build infrastructure into this bio body suit of ours at the various levels of being. When there is infrastructure, new infrastructure, what appears to happen is that spirit enters from a high domain. A hypothesis: it appears to need infrastructure to attach to.

When you say spirit, do you mean God or the source of intention?

Everything is God. It's a very high level of stuff that I label *spirit*. So when that enters to attach to infrastructure that we struggle for in life. That's what life is all about—building infrastructure into ourself. More spirit enters, and we become more conscious. As our consciousness grows, we see perspectives that we couldn't have imagined before. We see opportunities we couldn't have imagined before. We reach a place where we recognize that other people are all part of our larger self. *What we do to build another, we are building self.*

As we keep doing this work, we keep building this infrastructure; then more spirit enters and we become more conscious and we see other opportunities. We see other aspects of the universe. Going back to what you were saying about some people just not getting these things, it is because they are not conscious enough. They have not done enough work on themselves. I'll give you an example. When I was a young man I thought I knew all kinds of things about what we call God. Then eventually I became conscious enough to realize that I was not sufficiently conscious to truly understand what the concept "God" even meant. That's the way it is. We keep on keeping on and we keep growing.

I am going to ask you a bit of a philosophical question now. I will refer to your personal spiritual growth . . . have you found that when you do not follow your spiritual path, meaning doing what your intuitive self feels deep within, that you can bring upon yourself what I call a dark night of the soul? Like an experience that brings you to your knees, where there's nothing to do but open up and accept—or at least entertain the idea—that there might be something more?

Yes, the issue is . . . you are fortunate when the universe recognizes that you are ready for a transformation and you have a dark night of the soul experience. It takes you beyond where you were searching to understand that the old rhythm of your life's dance doesn't seem to work. You are plunged into feeling unplugged from reality. In my own case, that lasted for two years. At the end of two years I ended up all plugged back in again but I was lifted to a higher turn of the spiral of human development.

You were better and in bliss?

Yes. Conventional science was then a piece of cake.

Fred Alan Wolf once said to me, if you have a dark night of the soul, thank God, because it means there is light around the corner. But people don't realize this and they fight it keep themselves in misery.

Yes. It's an aspect of being willing to trust, willing to come to the view that the higher domains of the universe really know what they are doing because they are more conscious. They are doing things that you are not conscious of, so you cannot understand it at your level of reality. It requires a trust, requires that you are willing to put your ego in service to the larger whole.

I sometimes suggest that a person just do what the teacher says because the teacher says do it. Try it; see what happens.

Yes, try it. Experiment, it's an adventure. In life, you may choose to go through the crap in order to see the traps because you have chosen to make that your teacher. There are teachers beyond imagination; there is help beyond imagination, if you are willing to stretch yourself and become more than you were.

Let's move for a minute into physiology. Do you think that the brain thinks?

The brain is an output instrument from the thinking process which is at the level of mind, in my view. It is important to look at the unconscious versus the conscious. Tor Norretranders in Denmark wrote a very nice book called *The Users Illusion: Cutting Consciousness Down to Size*. When you look at the data, you see that the unconscious processes information at the rate of about 1,000,000 times that of the conscious. So the unconscious is doing all the work, all the heavy lifting. It takes—just at the five physical senses levels, and probably also at higher levels—the unconscious takes this data and processes it, manipulates it, probably makes calculations on it—sums, differences, and magnitudes—and then what it does is, it selects, fabricates, or edits and creates little kernels of information that it sends to the conscious mind. But, it sends them to the conscious only along channels that the conscious has heretofore given *meaning*. If the conscious does not give meaning to that information, it's dumped . . . or appears to be dumped. It's really the unconscious that's doing all this stuff, so in my modeling the unconscious functions at the second level of physical reality that we've discovered.

We've discovered two unique levels of physical reality with our experiments. The conventional one which is the electric atom/molecule level of physical reality particulate to nature; and the magnetic information wave, which comes from the physical vacuum. In general, these two are not coupled together and so the consciousness devices that *we* have created allow that coupling to occur. When you are coupled, every property measurement has at least these two levels of magnitude of effects. That is the conventional one that would give the normal properties and it would give our normal science. This second one is the magnetic information wave one and that magnitude can be positive or negative depending upon intention. That's the level of reality that is influenced by human intention. If there is not the consciousness there, which requires another substance whose existence I have postulated, if that isn't present, then these two levels of physical reality are totally uncoupled and all you get is conventional science. But when they are coupled, you need psychoenergetic science. You get new science and that's where you can manipulate the properties of material. You can influence technology.

Do you believe that physical reality is holographic?

I think everything beyond the coarse, physical level of reality is a wave domain; a frequency domain . . . and whenever you are dealing with frequencies and waves then you are dealing with diffraction processes and the core of diffraction processes is holography. So a hologram is a very natural way of representing a three-dimensional construct. But when you deal with higher domains, then of course you have many more dimensions to consider. I think the holographic concept is a very basic and important one for our future science.

You talk about this magnetic information wave and its positive and negative charges. Could this possibly have anything to do with "what goes around comes around"? We know that when you think a thought an electrical impulse is created in the brain and it jumps from synaptic gate to synaptic gate to synaptic gate. We also know that if we do live in a holographic environment, which quantum mechanics indicates, there is no separation from anything. So that mini lightning bolt in your brain doesn't consider itself confined within a skull, and it "goes somewhere". We know that molecules and atoms vibrate, oscillate . . . and when they do, they transmit and receive. Does this relate to transmitting positive information and receiving it back, and transmitting negative information and receiving it back?

Let's touch on that for a minute because all of the things you talked about are structures at the electric atom/molecule level of physical reality. If you look at the body—what we see—we are mostly electric in nature, at that level of reality. The movement of electric charge induces magnetic fields. The physical body, the coarse physical body, doesn't have symmetry between the electric and magnetic. We have electric monopoles, which are single electric charges. We have electric dipoles, which are a positive charge and negative charge bound together at short distances. We have magnetic dipoles. We don't have magnetic monopoles at the conventional level of physical reality. We have spent billions of dollars looking for magnetic monopoles at that level because physicists expect symmetry and they haven't found them. The conclusion they've reached is that magnetic monopoles don't exist.

Our work shows something quite different. Our work shows that if you condition the space using the kinds of devices we create, you lift the electromagnetic symmetry state and your instruments begin to access results that can only be interpreted in terms of having accessed magnetic monopoles. I would say by combining our work with what has been done in the search for magnetic monopoles in conventional reality, what you must say is that you cannot *access* magnetic monopoles from our normal electromagnetic symmetry state, called a U1) gauge symmetry, but that is a complex subject that I don't think we can go into now. We find, for example, experimentally, that once you condition a space using our consciousness devices, you can apply a magnetic field to that space or to a property measurement in that space, and from conventional reality, if you changed/inverted the magnetic field from positive to negative, then conventional reality would say it would be no different because the conventional reality—our normal U(1) gauge space—says that the magnetic potential depends on the square of the magnetic field and the magnetic force depends upon the gradient of that square of magnetic field. You shouldn't see any difference in the results of reversing the sign of the field.

However, in our experiments we find that if you reverse the magnetic field where you are measuring, for instance, the pH of water, we see big differences between whether the north pole is facing the water versus the south pole. In a conventional reality space, you don't see any difference, so the application of consciousness now has lifted this symmetry state to a place where magnetic monopoles function in that level of physical reality. In that level magnetic monopoles speak to function in this second level of physical reality. We've determined experimentally that that appears to occur at the vacuum level. Now, the vacuum level of physical reality occurs in the space between the fundamental particles that make up the atoms and molecules. It appears to be mostly empty space there and when we use the word "vacuum," what it really means is that there is no course physical substance there. The assumption is that there is nothing there; our work shows that is not true. There is other stuff which we have accessed.

Are you talking about the Zero Point Field?

No, the Zero Point Field . . . most people don't get this quite right. The Zero Point Field is what physicists defined a long, long time ago as behavior of absolute zero of temperature—zero degrees Celsius. Unlike in classical mechanics, in quantum mechanics you see that there is still a vibrational state at absolute zero temperature. That absolute zero temperature state is called the Zero Point State or the Zero Point Field. People who aren't careful with their language equate that with the vacuum level of physical reality.

This is in all of the interviews I've been conducting.

See that just confuses things. One has to discriminate one from the other.

Linguistics is a big problem.

We don't know the proper language. We haven't lived with this stuff long enough. In essence, we have a language of apples and we want to describe oranges.

For our readers, I think what you are saying is that yes, it can effect positive and negative. You have literally changed the pH in water up one point and down one point and, not only did you do that, you did it 3,000 miles away from where you had the water located.

Yes, our measurement accuracy was 1/100 pH units.

With only thought and intention?

Intention which we embed from a deep meditative state into a simple electronic device, and that device becomes the host for that intention which we can then ship by FedEx to the laboratory 1,500 miles away or 3,000 miles away or 10,000 miles away probably and they can have the apparatus set up. They just have to plug this into the wall outlet, switch it on and just wait and you will see the properties start to change after a month or so.

This is just a very small, simple device. It's not a big complicated instrument.

No, it's four integrated circuits. It's very simple. Its output power is less than 1,000,000th of a watt.

You just put it by the water and in a reasonably short period of time the pH went up or it went down, depending on the specific intention used.

If the room is not conditioned, it takes a while to condition the room to this higher symmetry level. When it's at this higher symmetry level you have coupling between these two levels of reality, and then the intention or the tuning of that device can influence this second level of reality. Then your instruments start to move in the direction of your intention and generally level off very much in the region of magnitude change associated with that specific intention.

It also supports the belief that human beings can do this with their mind.

Absolutely because they have the same infrastructure. They have this higher gauge symmetry state in their acupuncture meridian chakra systems. That's what our experiments showed with humans. The south pole of a magnet will strengthen muscle groups and the north pole of a magnet will weaken muscle groups. That's a DC magnetic field polarity effect, which cannot occur at normal physical reality. At that level you only have dipoles, magnetic dipoles. Whereas at this higher level you appear to have magnetic monopoles coexisting with electric monopoles, and that is a higher gauge symmetry state. It's also a higher thermodynamic free energy per unit volume state, and we have discovered a way to build instruments to measure that in a room where humans are.

You brought up the word muscle, which reminded me of the work Gary Schwartz was doing with the heart transplant.

There is infrastructure in the heart living in the individual.

If a heart from a donor is transplanted into person, then the recipient person's aspect of consciousness changes.

Some aspect of the recipient's consciousness will change because the heart has consciousness. All the structures have consciousness in them because we're living, conscious beings.

That would support why some mice that were anesthetized woke up more quickly because another mouse had been anesthetized earlier in that space.

Yes, because it is conditioning of the space and that's what we humans do and can do. We can do this thousands to millions of times more effectively than we have in the past.

Would that not indicate or support the fact that we can heal ourselves with our mind?

Yes, yes indeed. There is a lot of data to support that. Now we can do this kind of thing by embedding specific intentions for healing into a simple little device, ship it to someone a long way away, and they just plug it into their bedroom by their bed. They're soaking in that field as long as they sleep every day.

I actually did this with Dean Radin. I developed this little intention carrier. I think I told you I'm a medical intuitive and I read for Dean one day. He had something going on with his stomach that had been going on for about two years. I printed out his picture, set it on my desk, and placed the little frequency machine there . . . I hear numbers in my head that I assossiate with frequencies in the body. I put the number I got for Dean into the machine and set it there. Six weeks later Dean called and said his stomach was healed for the first time in two years.

Well, that is impressive. That's experimental data. The issue is to suspend disbelief and start studying it.

Do you believe that information is encoded within frequencies in mind, and then interpreted by brain?

Information is indeed encoded in frequencies, and there is information at multiple levels in the universe. There is the standard kind of information that is being encoded in a program using conventional electrical processes, and there is information at the next higher level, and the next higher level, etc. They get more and more powerful as you go up the rungs of the ladder of understanding. Yes, I think we will work more and more with this in the future. As we change that information, we will change the thermodynamic free energy, which means that we will create forces and do things with those forces.

In laymen's language, would that mean information is in frequencies kind of like Morse code, which the brain then interprets and responds to, and releases whatever chemicals/neurotransmitters into our bodies that make us feel what we feel?

Well, the issue is, the lowest level is doing that in the coarse physical body and the brain. What you call the brain, you are referring to just the . . . we'll call it the cosmic brain; the higher dimensional brain.

I hear people often say, "I placed an intention but nothing happened." Would you agree that intention is most powerful when you have a more cohesive, focused intention?

The more coherent you become when you hold an intention, a strong desire, to be fulfilled, the higher the probability you'll have of its happening. Swamis in India, who have trained themselves for a good part of their lives to be sufficiently inner-self managed—which means to be sufficiently coherent—can be quite good at this.

Let me give you an example. The best example of course is a laser. Let me use the example of a 60-watt light bulb. It shines a little bit of light but not a lot of light. The reason it doesn't shine a lot of light is because of what's called destructive interference of the wave; the photons coming out of the light bulb are not in phase with each other. However, with intention you could orchestrate those atoms creating the light in the core of the light bulb. If you could do that so that the photons would come out riding on each other's back in phase with each other, then you would have an energy density coming out from that light bulb which would probably be on the order of a 1,000 times the surface of the sun. Incredible potential exists there if you make things coherent.

If you are thinking many thoughts at one time, you are not in focused coherence. Would you agree with that?

Certainly.

Do you think that matter first forms in the etheric field, then to the level of quantum particles, decreasing in frequency as it manifests mass?

Yes, the "old etheric" is where the psychoenergetics phenomena occur. That's the template for the caurse physical reality that comes into existence because of the patterns placed in this frequency domain. I don't use the old usage . . . well, in the beginning I did use the word etheric, but it carries baggage, so I've developed another procedure where in essence if you produce coupling between these two unique levels of physical reality, you then move to a higher level of gauge reality where intention can work. If you reduce that coupling to almost zero, then you get a conventional gauge reality and you get our conventional physics. In essence, that's the way it is. You reproduce all of the normal physics if you uncouple these two domains of physical reality. There are still higher dimensional domains, and we will eventually discover a coupling with those domains. Without being strongly coupled, we will just have this second rung of the ladder.

Do you think the source of intention resides at the irreducible unit?

I think the source of intention exists in our spirit selves, as I said before, we are spirits having physical experience, so it is as if that is our core self. What is evolving is our soul. The physical reality in our bio body suits with these two layers . . . that is just a diving bell that lets us interface with space-time reality. So in essence it's a vehicle that we use to interface with this particular classroom.

Do you think the irreducible unit and the Zero Point Field are the same, or are they different?

I think there is some confusion there because when you talk about the Zero Point Field—we talked about this—that is absolute zero temperature stuff. At absolute zero you have a vibrational state of electromagnetic stuff.

Is that the vacuum?

No it's not. You see, it is the vibrational states of electric atoms and the electric atoms are not in the vacuum. The electric atoms are electromagnetic stuff. They are electric stuff basically and so the Zero Point Field was defined for the *absolute zero temperature response* of that kind of stuff. The vacuum underlies that, and other kinds of stuff function there.

Would that be the irreducible unit?

It's an irreducible unit; however, if you go to the higher dimensions—what we call beyond the course level of the physical vacuum—that stuff originally (probably) came out of the higher dimensional domains. So when you say irreducible unit, you may have to go very, very high up this ladder of understanding to find that stuff. We don't have the tools to effectively investigate there; we are incapable of making really good experiments of that level.

We need more funding.

Yes that's true, always. But the issue is, we can experience these things, and we can come to internally know in a subjective way, but to be able to have objective instrumental response . . . that's another story and that's what we ultimately have to get to. We just have to be patient with respect to that. We have to withhold course judgment and go forward. Just make it happen.

Do you believe we have complete free will?

Now, when we talk about free will, what that means is the freedom to make choices and in a democratic society, we have that big time. Maybe not 100 percent now—we keep losing it bit by bit—but nonetheless, it's making choices. How can you grow as a spiritual being without making choices? You have to learn to make the right choice.

Would that be the equivalent of saying we have the ability to place intention.

Yes, yes, exactly. The superposition of all of those intentions in the now influence the next picture of our future. They become the reality.

*Through placing intention, we can't guarantee it will happen, but
through placing intention we do have the ability to change the potential possibilities.*

Right indeed. I think we create our future collectively by the
intentions we make in the now and made in the past. The *means*
we use to fulfill our intention creates the kind of future we have to
live in.

*Psychoenergetics is a new word; would you tell us what you mean
by that before we end?*

The foundation for psychoenergetics really began in the Soviet
Union. People who wanted to do work in that area had to make
it seem and sound scientific rather than theological in order to
actually have the freedom to pursue it. So, *psycho-* is, of course, of
the psyche, and *energy* is the energetics. So basically, it dealt with
energies of living humans, and therefore made it palatable to their
Soviet masters.

There were manifestations of great human abilities: levitation,
mind reading, precognition, healing, etc., etc., so all these things
are associated with the human psyche and consciousness, human
consciousness. Here is where the separation from traditional science comes in. In traditional science you could write an equation on a blackboard which is mass with arrows back and forth to
energy, and pretty much all the work of traditional science for the
last 400 years could be encapsulated in that metaphor. The connection between the mass and energy is Einstein's E=MC squared.
Since the days of Descartes the unstated assumption in science has
been that no human qualities of consciousness, intention, emotion, mind, or spirit can significantly influence a well-designed target experiment in physical reality. So, psychoenergetics flies in the
face of that unstated assumption, which may have been correct in
those old days, but it is certainly not correct now. And psychoenergetics expands that metaphorical equation where now we have
matter's arrows back and forth to energy and arrows back and forth
to information and arrows back and forth to consciousness.

*When you say consciousness, can that be replaced with aware-
ness, or do you mean the energy of all there is?*

I think something remarkably different than the present definition for consciousness as awareness or awakeness. To me, the
problem with the word consciousness is that none of us have come
to an agreed upon definition of the term. And perhaps it is because
the term is basically so broad. For example, I think of human consciousness as a byproduct of spirit entering dense matter, which is
us. Now, it's probably better not to ask what consciousness is at this
point in time, because we know so little about it. So let's just ask
the question, what does consciousness do?

As soon as you do that you immediately realize that consciousness manipulates information—information in the form of a set
of numbers to make sums and dividends and multiplicans, etc., or
the integration of . . . let's say you have a table top with a bunch of
letters separated on it and they are all a-jumble. But you rearrange
them in the form of words and the words in the form of a sentence,
so there is *meaning*. You've produced a great deal of order and the
order has *meaning*. And that is *information*.

We find we do the same thing if we collect a set of symbols and
put them into master equations that drive our present engineering
and our science. Or it can be the kind of thing you do on a lovely
Sunday afternoon when you pull a box down from the shelf and it's
a jigsaw puzzle. And you arrange these oddly formed pieces often
into some of the most beautiful pictures. That's creating information out of disorder.

Now, we've known for at least sixty years that a process in
nature that increases the information content actually produces a
decrease in the entropy in the universe. And you can simply think
of this as creating more order. Well, that's important and there is
a mathematical equation connecting these two. Now, we've also
known for one-hundred-fifty years that it is the thermodynamic
free energy process in nature that drives all the processes; all the
things we've ever learned are due to a change in the thermodynamic free energy. And when you look at that thermodynamic
free energy function it has in it three main terms. The first one is

pressure-volume. The second one is plus the internal energy. The third one is minus temperature times the entropy.

Now, in the old days we used the pressure volume term to drive steam engines. And today we use them to drive compressors for refrigerators and other such things. The energy term the general public knows most commonly is when we accelerate fundamental particles in special reactors and drive them into particular materials to create a kind of micro explosion in which all kinds of particles come out. And we've learned a great deal about fundamental particles in nature over the last seventy-five years from this kind of work. So, that's a real bashing of things together.

In the last term—this temperature times entropy—if the entropy is constant but the temperature differs, you can get geothermal energy out of the earth by the temperature difference at the surface and something deep down. And we're doing that in order to make an energy resource. And the other one is where the temperature is constant now and there is a change in the entropy driven by the increase of information in the process. Here one might go into a deep meditative state and invoke the physical vacuum or deeper levels of the vacuum and invite nature to reveal itself in special ways, and that changes the thermodynamic driving force so that a process can go on in the physical vacuum that reveals to us more about the nature of nature.

So that's psychoenergetics. It deals with these things largely in the human psyche because the human psyche now can drive processes in the human. It can by working on this within self to become inner self-managed at the more subtle levels. It produces a kind of order within oneself and as one does, one increases the thermodynamic free energy in the universe. One restores the potential that drives our world. One can do this kind of thing by directed, focused intention. And one can change from a normal individual to an adept. And, if one continues that, one can convert oneself from an adept to being a master. And if one continues doing that one can change from being a master to being an avatar.

So there is huge potential in the future for humanity to do this inner work within ourselves and evoke changes at the vacuum level of reality so as to do many, many things. To make us more and more capable, to create new technologies, to change the errors we've made in our world from the past perspective, from the traditional science perspective. All of this is related to consciousness. We are really just starting to come to a world where our consciousness can deal with other levels of reality and have very big effects. The effect of consciousness in our present electric atom molecule world is basically very small because of the form of the equation that connects information and entropy. Information change and entropy change. So it's all about changes.

I want to make sure I understand you. Are you saying that by entering an altered state of mind and placing focused intention, people can affect physical reality and heal themselves or change their paths or change the things that are happening in their lives and be more creative and successful?

All of the above. The issue is what you focus on with sustained intention is what you become.

Back in 1997, I took an unstated assumption of orthodox science that no human consciousness, intention, emotion, mind, or spirit could significantly influence a target experiment in physical reality. This has been the assumption of science since the days of Descartes. So I said to myself, I don't think that's true, but let's do the experiment. Let's do a serious experiment to see in our present world if that is still true. Was it ever true? I don't know . . . but was it still true?

So we designed four separate, unique experiments—well designed; well monitored. And we had them running, and they gave traditional electric atom molecule physical results that all the scientists are familiar with. Then we added intention to the picture. I didn't do it using humans, because that had been done before and humans are basically not reliable at this stage of their development. They can't sustain and replicate exactly the same level of intention all the time. So I went through two steps. The first step was to take a simple electronic circuit, a little black box if you like, and have four people go into the deep meditative state, and then a specific intention for one of the experiments would be stated and held by all four at the same time. We were working with one black box in which we were embedding human intention to affect a particular experiment.

We designed four experiments, so we eventually had four black boxes—all of which are the same. Embedded in them from a deep meditative state is a specific intention. What you do is you take that particular black box into a room where the particular experiment is being run, place it about a foot or two from the experiment, plug it into the wall socket, and turn it on. Its electrical output power is less than one-millionth of a watt—a very, very small amount of electric power. The frequency of the output radiation is in the one- to ten-million hertz range. So, it's the microwave range, but very, very weak.

What we intended to see—and what we did see for these four unique experiments—was that there would be a slow change from the background and when I say slow, nothing much happened for the first month. Then the property measurements started to change, always in the direction of the intention. It would rise and after maybe another month it would start to plateau, generally very much in the level of the specific intention. We found we could take water—for example, purified water—and increase its pH, which is the acid/ alkaline balance of the water, by one full pH unit. Now one pH unit is a lot for a biological system. If we were doing this in the human body, let's say in the blood, and we increased it a half a pH unit or decreased it a half a pH unit, the human would be dead or dying. So, for a biological system, one full pH unit is a very great deal. So the intention was to do this with no chemical additions, and the water is just in equilibrium with air. We were remarkably successful with this. The next experiment was to take the same water and the intention in the black box was to reduce the pH by one full pH unit with no chemical additions and again it's in equilibrium with air. We were very successful with that. And we can do that with all kinds of water. We're changing the chemistry of the system—a kind of modern-day alchemy.

How long did it take the people to place the intention?

Generally we do it twice. A full cycle might be a half an hour. And I generally always like to do a repeat. So it takes an hour to an hour and a half. Our experience is that we can do maybe four of these a day. And we're very tired at the end. But in essence that's sort of a timeline, at least with the sort of devices that we had. They're not as good as the devices I want to make. But they were sufficient to do these four experiments and to replicate one of them around the world.

Can anyone do this? Or do they have to get in an altered state—a very cohesive, focused state.

Well I haven't studied that; I'll leave that for others. But basically everyone has the latent capability, the internal capability, to do it. But in our case, all four people were well accomplished meditators. They could go into a deep state and sustain it for a long period of time with a specific intention and with specific visualization. That generally takes practice to do that. And my feeling always was, the unseen does the heavy lifting. I mean, I've asked many great healers what is special about their abilities, and they generally say they don't particularly do anything; they just try to be as clear a channel as they can for the universe to work through them. So we try to do just that kind of thing, and you can feel the connection with the unseen. That was most remarkable for us when I wanted to imprint ten at once to do the simplest kind of experiment. I was doing this with Norm Shealy. We wanted to do it with ten subjects. When we imprinted these ten, we did them all at once. So we stacked them up on the table, hooked them all up together and did it. And during that meditation, the energy flow through us was absolutely palpable; it was so strong, there could be no doubt that something was working through us into this world.

What about the repeatability you've had happen about the world?

That's interesting. We first selected five sites in this country, and the people who put up half the money for the work wanted there to be a control site within two to twenty miles of the local device-active sites. Later on there were two additional international sites—one in London, one in Milan, Italy. But initially we picked three sites—one was our Payson lab site, one was in Missouri, and one was in Kansas. There were two other U.S. sites—one in Bethesda, and one in Baltimore. The Baltimore site was at the NIH, and the Bethesda site was in the uniformed services hospital. So the first thing we did was with the three initial sites. We provided equipment that was shipped to them directly from the manufacturing center and purified water that was shipped to them from Fisher Scientific. We showed them how to set it up, and they ran background data for about three months. And when we were convinced they knew what to do, we had them ship us the diskettes of their data streams. We were measuring three parameters. One was pH, one was air temperature, and one was water temperature. And another actually turned out to be the electrode voltage. So they shipped us their diskettes by snail mail. We didn't want there to be much digital interaction.

By the end of the three months we then delivered them a black box which was to increase the pH by one full pH unit. That is, one black box for each of the three stations that were running the background. And what we saw was exactly what I described earlier. We plugged it in, turned it on; nothing much was seen in the first month. And then it started to change. We picked the example of the pH increasing, and we would see the measured pH going up and we would see that it plateaued. If we took the device away before it plateaued it would just slowly decay over several months. But if we let it go to the plateau level which was something like two to three months later, then the measurements thereafter, at least for a couple of years that we continued looking at it, would be at this upper level. So it was a very, very interesting and very successful result.

Now the thing that was strange was that at our control sites, which had exactly the same equipment, but didn't have this black box, we got the same results. That was really strange. I then had to go back to a first observation. After our very first imprinting of one of these black boxes with the water pH going up, we found right after we had done that, I put an unimprinted device and an imprinted device about a hundred meters away from each other. And I turned them both *off* electrically. Okay, so nothing should happen, right? Wrong! It turns out that within three to five days the unimprinted device had picked up the imprint from the imprinted device. I was shocked; dismayed. I realized that I wouldn't be able to do the kind of experiments I wanted to do because these two had somehow become entangled with each other, and the imprint transfers, so we've lost our control.

Two things then occurred to me. One is "holy moly," here we have evidence that there is at least one other communication channel in the universe whereby information can transfer from one thing to another. That's remarkable. And the second was, I have got to find a way to keep the imprint intention in the device for long enough to do experiments and have others do experiments. I reasoned . . . well, maybe electromagnetism is involved. So I wrapped the device in aluminum foil. That would block out all the optical range EM information. And I then put the device in a small electrically grounded Faraday cage, which would block out all the gigahertz or megahertz radio wave electromagnetics down to about 1,000 hertz. One can't do much below that because it takes too much copper shielding, but when I did that I found then that I could keep the imprint intention in the device for about three to six months. So that meant that we could really do experiments, and we could have other people do experiments.

Did you ever fool with using magnetisms or polarity?

We tried many, many things. Nothing shields this radiation, really.

Would it push it harder to use magnetism?

We have done experiments where we have built magnetically shielded boxes five feet cubed to do experiments in. We used new metal shielding, and inside we used thick nu-metal containers. And this energy just goes right through. The mu-metal doesn't shield. That was remarkable. What it means is it's just like the experiment that I did with an unimprinted device and imprinted device a hundred meters apart and electrically turned off.

So it doesn't have to be turned on to work?

They are entangled. So the point is the control sites were two to twenty miles away. They were information-entangled with the black box site. So I call these IIEDs: Intention Imprinted Electrical Devices. We thought okay, we know now that it isn't just 100 meters, but at two to twenty miles they can be information-entangled. So I decided let's use the Baltimore and Bethesda sites as the control sites for the Payson, Missouri, and Kansas sites. So we had the Baltimore and Bethesda sites run background with never one of these IIEDs there in that location—at least at that time. And we found that after two months the pH at those sites had gone up about 0.85 pH units. There never was one of these devices there. So that says the information entanglement extends over something of the order of 1,500 miles. Then I had interaction with a young group of scientists in London, and another group of scientists in Milan. I never met these folks. But they wanted to get involved and do something. So I said OK, why don't you purchase this equipment and set it up this way and run background. Well, the English site went online first and within three weeks, with no black box there, the pH went up one full pH unit.

Three months later the Milan site went online and within one week the pH had gone up one pH unit, and within three weeks it had gone up 1.7pH units. Then I looked back at the old data and the control site at Missouri had also gone up 1.7pH units, and it was below ground. Then I looked at the data much more carefully and found that the sites where the pH unit had gone up 1.7 pH units were both below ground. The Milan site was in a basement. And the sites that had gone up 1 pH unit were all at ground level. And the Baltimore and Bethesda sites were three stories up in the air, and they went up 0.85 pH units. This seems to suggest that whatever this energy is, it prefers to go through the ground than through the air. Electromagnetism prefers to go through the air than through the ground. So that was interesting.

Would that mean it has something to do with the magnetism in the earth?

Perhaps . . . but basically, I did an experiment that related to magnetism in a very important way because all of these things that I mentioned were just sort of a first phase. The second phase of the work was to try to figure out what was going on . . . why were these things happening? What was the different physics, if there was different physics?

We had noticed there were three characteristic signatures associated with these experiments. The first one was this information entanglement that I just talked about, because now we see the information entanglements are between macroscopic sites like a laboratory of 10,000 cubic feet and another laboratory 6,000 miles away of the order of 1,000 cubic feet, and all at room temperature. Well this is very, very different than quantum entanglement. But it's a real phenomenon with a range of at least 6,000 miles. So it's definitely not electromagnetism. It's something else.

Another level of reality.

Another level of reality, another aspect of reality. The telling experiment for me was one where we did use a magnet. We put it underneath the pH vessel, the little cylindrical jar that holds the water, and we had the measurement instruments coming in at the top. Underneath it we put a disk magnet—a big ceramic magnet, about two inches in diameter and about a quarter of an inch thick. We stuck it under the jar, centrally symmetric. We left one of the poles, let's say the north pole, up for three to five days, and then we just turned it over and left the south pole *up* for three to five days and measured continuously.

Now if you do that experiment in a normal electric/atom molecule level of reality, you don't see any difference, because in our normal level of reality there are only magnetic dipoles. The effect we got was, we found that the magnetic south pole *up* strongly increased the pH—it became more alkaline—and the magnetic north pole *up* strongly decreased the pH; became more acidic. These are little magnets of maybe 100 gauss to 500 gauss, very much like the ones you put on your refrigerator. So it's a very small field, relatively speaking. Large still compared to the earth because the Earth's magnetic field is only a half a gauss. So larger than that, but people are doing experiments these days at a million gauss, many millions of gauss. So in any event, we saw this difference with the DC magnetic, with the polarity change. And that cannot occur in our normal reality, because with dipoles the magnetic force and the magnetic energy are independent of the polarity. But here we saw a difference. This tells us that the kind of magnetism in this new phenomena is important, and it can't be a dipole field. The only way you get this kind of effect is if you have monopoles or an odd number of single poles . . . that is south or north. So that became truly important at a *fundamental* level of physics.

So now we come to the point you were starting to make, being, that we have accessed another level of reality, and I will call it another level of physical reality. Because our subsequent work indicates it comes from the physical vacuum. That is, the vacuum level of reality in my modeling and description occurs in the space between the fundamental particles that make up the atom. If you take the old classical picture of electrons taking orbits around the nucleus, most of the volume of the atom is empty space. The particles take up very little space and their orbits take up very little space. So, all of that other space is the vacuum. Like the kind of thing you have in outer space . . . or better than that, but still, that's the issue. So this kind of thing is coming from the vacuum level of reality.

So let's suppose that, indeed, I'm correct that we've touched a magnetic monopole level of reality. I call it magnetic information wave levels of reality. And suppose we could turn the strength of it up just by turning a dial. When it's *not* turned up the electrons just go take their orbits and they just go on and on and on in the same way. But as you turn the magnetic monopole factor up, you pass a critical place where you now think you start to see a change in the locus of the electrons in their orbits. If you turn it up higher, we think you see a greater divergence . . . and turning it up even higher shows even more. So what you see is the effect of an attractor, which is the way traditional physics talks about what is going on in the universe with dark energy and dark matter. The dark matter is acting like an attractor. They don't see it directly, but they see its effects on other electric atom molecule stuff like planets and so on.

So now we come to the results of all of our experiments, and that is, we have discovered that there are two unique levels of physical reality. In one of them is the electric atom/molecule level, and the second one is the magnetic information wave level. So that any property measurements, let's call it magnitude Q sub m, meaning measurement is equal to Q sub E, which means the electric atom/molecule level, the normal thing we see in a laboratory experiment of this kind, plus alpha effective, which is a coupling coefficient, times Q sub M, which is a magnetic information wave level, which functions in the physical vacuum. And alpha effective is the coupler between the two.

Normally, under normal conditions, these two levels of reality are uncoupled. So all we get is the electric atom molecule stuff. That's the typical stuff that traditional science measures in its laboratory every day. But through the use of consciousness in this device, which is switched on in the environment, something coming out of the device, which is really the coupler material that comes out and fills the room and fills the instruments so that now there becomes a coupling, so that the instruments now can begin to access this other stuff, this magnetic stuff. Without this coupler substance, which is related to our embedding the intention in the device and the unseen universe doing something also with that device, which relates to that coupler stuff, we wouldn't see those results. But we do see them. And we see them every time.

We see them in the replication experiments because we've also discovered a way to quantitatively measure the effect of this device. That is, we are able to experimentally see the excess thermodynamic free energy for the proton, which is really the hydrogen ion, when you're making pH measurements. What you're measuring there is the H+ ion, essentially. So what I was able to do was to expand our normal thermodynamics to include this next term, which was like a magnetic monopole term, and a magnetic potential brought about by this process. And when I did that we found that experimentally we could analyze the pH measurement data. We could tell when we departed from normal reality in pH terms, and we could measure how far we were departed or how far the space was elevated with respect to this new thermodynamic potential. And we could measure it, and we measured it for all ten sites involved in our replication experiments. Even though we had never been there, it was all in the diskettes of the information. And now of course we're doing experiments all the time to see the effects of human biofields and such on a room. A room can be converted into a sacred space, just like in some European cathedrals, by humans.

We found when we looked more deeply that humans have their acupuncture meridian chakra system at this coupled level of reality. Let me go back to the kind of equation I tried to write on this imaginary blackboard that is Q sub M is equal to Q sub e+alpha effective times Q sub m. When alpha effective is close to zero, and that's our normal reality, all you get is the Qe+aeff part of the equation. This shows that consciousness is very much different than awareness, because, in the consciousness embedded device, the alpha effective increases from about zero. It increases to a level where now we produce coupling. So we go from the uncoupled state of physical reality, where these two kinds of universes are there but they cannot interact with each other, to where, with consciousness, they can begin to interact with each other. You see the property measurements change. So, that's an effect of consciousness in the form of human intention and maybe something else on reality.

I have a couple of questions here from Jim Beal, and I'd like you to tell me after you answer his questions what this means for mankind. Jim's really into EMF fields, and he wants to know if EMF fields affect the ability of the intender or the device?

My response is that there is probably a reaction equation that occurs between electromagnetism and magneto-electrism. Magneto-electrism is this magnetic charge moving to create electric fields, just like electromagnetism is an electric charge moving to create magnetic fields. But they are quite different. They have a different photon that is involved in the process. It has to be. We can easily shield electromagnetism. We have no capability yet to shield magneto-electrism.

What about the pulsing of EMF fields? Is that what you're talking about?

No, it doesn't have to be pulsed fields which would create only magnetic *dipole* fields. But basically, I expect a similar kind of thing to occur in a general sense with magneto-electrism. And we're doing experiments to learn about that versus electromagnetism. The way Jim should begin to look at this is to think of a normal electrodynamic circuit. If it's a transformer, you can put in a secondary circuit and you can change the voltage and current relationship that occurs when you do that. Well in this case you take the analog electric circuit of our traditional electric atom/ molecule aspect of reality. And when you produce coupling, it's just like introducing a magneto-electric circuit where the elements of the secondary circuit are just opposites to what they are in the electric circuit. A resistor is probably still a resistor of some kind. But a capacitor, which is electric charge storage, will be magnetic charge storage in the other level and an inductor at the electric level will be a capacitor in the magneto-electric circuit. So you can begin to see the coupling produce interactive changes. But it's not straightforward. There are lots of things to learn, and we're about trying to learn those things. But that's the way I am presently looking at this coupling.

We found with humans that if you do a kinesiological study for various kinds of points in the body (and we used a world-class kinesiologist), if you bring a bar magnet into the near field, the south pole strengthens that particular muscle and the north pole weakens that muscle. Since it's a DC magnetic field polarity effect, it says that the human body (maybe all vertebrates) has a system in their bodies that is at the coupled level of reality. And the coupled level of reality is a higher thermodynamic free energy state, which means it can drive all processes at our normal electric atom molecule level. That is the uncoupled state, and most of the human body is at that level. Otherwise our biology and our medicine wouldn't be the way it is. That's particularly interesting.

When you look at muscles . . . it turns out that there are proprioceptors in muscles, and there is a very weak kind of coupling between proprioceptors and the acupuncture meridian system. So it allows higher dimensional energies to come through into the acupuncture meridian system. Because it's at the coupled level of reality, human intention can influence it. Then you can get qi-gong masters to pump energy into the normal electric atom molecule level of the body, and therefore affect biology and human health. All humans ultimately can do this kind of thing if they work at it. It requires training, like any athlete.

It opens the door to some new free energy.

Yes. Let me give you an idea of what's available. For quantum mechanics and relativity theory to be internally self-consistent, people like Wheeler and others calculated that the vacuum, the coarse physical vacuum has to contain an energy density of about the equivalent of 10 to the 94 grams equivalent per cc. That's a huge amount of energy. But let's put it in terms that we can understand. Let's do two particular calculations. One is, we know the electric mass density everywhere in the universe. The astronomers have worked that out and we can get a kind of average mass density. So we could multiply that average mass density by the volume of the universe. Let's take a sphere 15 billion light years in radius, and we multiply it by the average mass density. That gives us how much electric mass there is in the cosmos that we know of. And you multiply each gram by E=MC squared. So that gives the total amount of electric energy stored in the mass of our universe. On the other hand let's take a calculation of just a single hydrogen atom volume. It has a radius of about ten one billionths of a centimeter, and we calculate the volume, and it's something of the order of 10 to the minus 24 cubic centimeters, a very small number. And we multiply that now by the 10 to the 94 grams per cc that's supposed to be in the vacuum. And we compare the two. What you see is that the energy, the vacuum energy storage in the single hydrogen atom is a trillion times that of all the electric mass energy stored in our physical cosmos. Now you can begin to see some idea of what kind of latent potential energy exists in the coarse physical vacuum, and perhaps what I think will become available energy as we go forward in our evolution. And we will see how important the physical vacuum and our understanding of this vacuum are to us.

One point is that our discussion tonight shows you that consciousness is a hell of a lot more than just awareness.

Yes, yes.

CHAPTER 6

Henry Stapp, Ph.D.

Henry Stapp did his doctoral work under the direction of Nobel Laureates Emilio Segre and Owen Chamberlain. He created the theoretical framework for the analysis of the scattering of polarized protons, and then analyzed the data obtained from the experiments at the Lawrence Radiation Laboratory at the University California in Berkeley, obtaining the phase shifts first at 360 MEV and later at higher energies. His work was the first large-scale computer analysis in high-energy physics. Subsequently he worked closely with Wolfgang Pauli in Zurich on parity violations, and on fundamental problems in quantum theory, He wrote there an essay entitled "Mind, Matter, and Quantum Mechanics," which developed into a book of the same title, published thirty-five years later. He has written over 300 technical and mathematical published papers pertinent to basic foundational issues. During the sixties he was a principal mathematical and philosophical spearhead of new approach to quantum theory known as S-Matrix theory. He worked in Munich with Heisenberg on the problem of the interpretation of quantum theory, and later in Austin with Wheeler on the same subject. His paper, "The Copenhagen Interpretation," is widely recognized as a seminal work on this subject. In 1968 he wrote his first paper about the apparent need in quantum theory for faster-than-light transfer of information. This issue had been raised in the paper about the Einstein-Podolsky-Rosen "paradox" published in 1964 by John Bell. His most recent works focus on the strong influence of quantum processes on the working of the brain, and specifically on the fact that quantum theory brings conscious choices by human agents irremovably into the physical theory in a way that directly accounts for the ability of a person's conscious choices to causally influence the activity in his or her physical brain. He is also the author of *Mind, Matter and Quantum Mechanics* and *Mindful Universe: Quantum Mechanics and the Participating Observer.*

Eva: Please tell us a little bit about yourself before we get started.

Henry: I am a physicist at Lawrence Berkley Laboratory, University of California, and in principal I am an elementary particle physicist . . . theoretical physicist. Recently my interests have been on the problem of the interaction of the mind—namely our conscious thoughts or subjective experiences—and our brain; the relationship between mind and brain. My thesis is that quantum has a great deal to do with it. You cannot really understand the connection within the classical physics where the brain is regarded as a bunch of particles basically moving around and there is no way of understanding how consciousness can come out of bouncing billiard balls, so to speak. On the other hand, quantum theory is designed to be a theory of relationships between our experiences and it is coarsely tied into mathematical descriptions of a physical nature that are designed to connect and form relationships between experiences. So, quantum theory provides an appropriate and beautiful way of understanding the connection between mind and brain. I have a book entitled, *The Mindful Universe: Quantum Mechanics and the Participating Observer.*

When you talk about consciousness, what is your definition of that word?

You can define things in various ways and one way is to point out examples. You can point out examples of automobiles and things like this and I think most people know what their flow-of-consciousness experiences are—the experience of pain, joy, happiness, sorrow . . . all sorts of feelings. In psychology these are sometimes called the stream of consciousness. The stream of conscious thoughts—or thoughts, ideas, and feelings—is what people in this field refer to as mind . . . the stream of conscious thoughts. Brain on the other hand is something that is made up of neurons and other physically described substances located within your skull. These two things are described in quite different languages. Neurons are described in a physical language and also in a mathematical language as physics. Conscious experiences are described in terms of psychological concepts as thoughts, ideas, and feelings in general.

To add one more leg to that, you are not saying that consciousness is simply the opposite of being asleep. Some people think that. I guess that is a good definition for that limited perspective.

When you go to sleep in a sound, dreamless sleep, you are not having conscious experiences. People characterize consciousness as the difference between being awake and alert and having conscious experiences, and being asleep, where you have no conscious experiences. I don't think there is any conflict between those two ways of characterizing.

Mind is essentially for conscious experiences. Consciousness and mind, the way I use the term, are essentially the same; just two ways of referring to the same thing, namely your streams of conscious experiences. Mind is just one word that identifies those things.

Would you agree with me that we have three levels of awareness: sensate, cognitive, and self?

Yes, I think there are three things that can be present in your stream of consciousness—at least three things—and certainly those are three of them.

Is there more that you know of that I did not mention?

I am not sure how a feeling of anguish fits into your category; maybe it does. Any sort of experience you have; love, joy, hate, and things that come immediately through your senses. You have also things that are perhaps more subtle. In any case we certainly want to include anything that you're subjectively conscious of, or anything that is in your flow of consciousness.

What do you believe to be the source of intention?

I consider intention an aspect of certain of your experiences. Certain of your experiences have intentionality in the sense that you are intending to do something—your meaning, your goal of doing something—and certainly it comes in part from the brain. What your brain is doing has an affect or an influence on all of your thinking, and the question is, can it be completely characterized and described and understood just in terms of what your brain is doing? Or is there some origin or part of the origin also in things that are not completely described in terms of brain activity? In other words, do things we think causes experiences completely described in terms of brain activity? Or do we have something more general that has two ways of describing different aspects of the reality—one being the psychological description, and the other being the physical description—and if you have these two aspects of the underlying reality, then your intentions—like your other thoughts—could very well have origins, partial origins, in both of these aspects.

Is consciousness a process? If so, what do you believe to be its active agent? Is it just awareness, sensate, or cognitive?

As we experience our life, we understand what we mean by our flow of conscious experiences. The elements of this stream of consciousness are our conscious thoughts, so they are part of the reality, and they certainly have origins in things that have come before in the creation of a factual universe; the past. Presumably, if nature really has aspects that can be described in terms of psychological ideas, in terms of experiences— and also aspects that can be described in terms of physical description, mathematical descriptions in terms of physical ideas, the origin of your present conscious experiences—your flow of consciousness at the moment could very well have origins coming partly from psychological and partly from physical aspects of what has come before.

Do you think there are gradients of consciousness?

What do you mean by that?

Is it hierarchical?

Certainly intentions to do something like lift a heavy stone . . . you can feel a difference in the intensity there. There can be a more intense effort. You try and lift the stone and the effort you are applying is not great enough and so there is a quantitative aspect here. You might call it gradients: more and less. You can apply more effort and perhaps you can lift the heavy stone. In that sense there is the quantitative aspect that you feel more or less effort.

Classical science is not listening right now about intention and the holographic environment. Different people have different levels of awareness of understanding, and trying to talk to some of them about this is like talking to a wall sometimes. We're talking about gradients of conscious awareness. People perceive, understand, and accept things differently. Even if something has been presented as fact, they deny it, though the evidence is right in front of them. People don't understand mystical experiences until they have one, and then it changes their perception somewhat. How would quantum theory explain that, or would it support that . . . or do you know?

I think the fact that different people understand things differently doesn't mean anything in particular. I mean, we have all grown up learning things differently; we have different life experiences, and this is a complex subject extending back 2,000 years. There is a tremendous amount of material out there in literature that people can read, with many different points of view. Most of the philosophers of the past have addressed these questions, and we are now faced with having the advantage of a lot of technical data from neuroscience, and on the other hand the brain is a very complicated system. It's not to be expected that everyone would immediately have the same opinion.

How do you think that intention is carried out? What makes it come to be?

I think intentionality, the intentional aspect of your experiences, like if I intend to raise my arm, or I intend to steer my car in a certain direction or whatever . . . according to William James (probably the most famous American psychologist and philosopher), your intentions arise from your brain. Due to a situation in which you find yourself, the brain puts up a certain thought, a certain idea, of what you ought to do in this situation, and so the initial thought, feeling, or intention, according to William James, arises actually from brain activity . . . and the contribution to that from something beyond activity, known as consciousness, seems to hold this idea in place. There is a kind of two-fold causal situation—first the brain throws up a certain idea that you should, under the present circumstances, act in a certain way, according to William James. Then quantum theory—the consciousness aspect—is also able to keep this idea in place for longer than would be the case without the intervention of the conscious thoughts. Quantum theory explains in a very neat way how this really could come about, and in a way that fits a lot of data. It's a two-fold causation with intention and with holding in place of intention so that they actually result in actions.

I want to get clear on this. Does the brain think or does it just process? Does it actually create—does it have creativity—or does it process?

You have to understand what the brain is, or is supposed to be, according to physics. According to classical physics the brain is particles, which are just tiny bits of matter—hard bits of matter moving around—and some forces that are causing these tiny particles to move around. That's the old classical picture of what the brain is. Quantum theory has a completely different picture of what both the brain and the physical world in general are made up of. According to quantum mechanics, quantum physics, the actual structure of nature is made up of psychophysical events, namely, events that have both a psychological aspect and physical aspect, with the physical aspect being in some sense a reflection in the physical world of the experiential, or psychological, aspect. From this point of view the brain is, according to quantum ideas, really a sequence of events that has within it both psychological and physical aspects. Every actual part of the brain has a psychological aspect so it doesn't really have to throw it up. What is happening is that there is a sequence of events, each of which has a psychological aspect, so it is part of the brain's natural function to have in principle psychological aspects.

Some of these aspects which are probably best understood are feelings of one sort or another. Some of them rise to the level of consciousness and some, even though perhaps best understood as feelings, are still below the level of conscious awareness. The up side of all this is that your brain naturally generates things that are best described as feelings and some of these are well organized, powerful, and complex enough and have the necessary structure to be conscious feelings. The brain automatically produces these things, and you, the person with that brain, find yourself in some situation, and the brain goes to work to create an appropriate response to your situation . . . and this response will often contain conscious experiences.

Where does the brain get its information? Is the information contained within the physical body of the brain or is it contained within a wave or frequency field?

Given that the brain is what I just described it to be, namely it's the sequence of psychophysical events that have occurred in the past, and there are causal laws that transfer the intentions and information from the past to the present, the causal chain here involves the transmission of both the psychological and the physical aspects of the earlier events forward in time, and your later experiences are a consequence of the way your brain integrates the order of information in order to produce a new psychophysical event.

When you get an idea, the entire thought drops into the mind in one complete idea. It's not something where you say: "Oh, I need to think about this and figure it out," it just comes, all at one time. Mystics seem to have—or maybe they pay more attention to—this occurrence more often than most people. Where does that come from?

These events are whole events already. This is what is called a threshold effect. Namely that all of your experiences, all of your perceptions come—as William James said back 100 years ago—totally, or not at all. The whole unified thought appears as a unified thought. That's the way all thought comes to us.

Where does it come from?

You can answer this from two points of view. One is, what does contemporary science say about it? When you ask these "why questions," contemporary science probably does not give an adequate or full answer. There is an elaboration of what scientists have found, which was created by Alfred North Whitehead, and he actually describes what he believes to be the structure by which these events form themselves out of the facts and experiences from the past.

When you say from the past, do you mean from the individual's past or the past of all there is?

I mean in the global sense. According to this picture, reality is created by a sequence of events that are occurring and each one fixes certain facts to be *this*, not *that*, and in association with a psychological element, so you can think of the evolving structure of the universe as being created. Once these events have occurred, then they are in the past, and you have fixed past facts that constitute the history of the world. Then you have the process that's now happening, which is based upon what has happened in the past and the laws that relate to what has happened in the past to potentiality—to what is going to be happening now. When I say the past, I mean things have already been fixed by this process that creates the factual universe.

Do you think that we live in a holographic environment? Is that the way physical reality is experienced?

Certainly your experiences come from combining various elements from the past that come often from different locations, so in that sense spatially separated facts in the past get combined to form a new factual element in the present. If that is what you mean by holographic mainly, but a distribution in the past is contributing to the formation of the present then that is pretty understandable. I mean, we all understand even in ordinary experience how different influences from different places in the past can converge and cause the present reaction, whatever it might be. So in that sense, even non-mystical ordinary thought would say that yes, in that sense we have a holographic universe.

If you want to talk about holography as a technical thing having to do with certain laws of optics then that's a much more subtle thing and the extent to which that holds is probably in the way one would pose it. To what extent is, for example, memory in the brain? For example, Karl Pribram, when he talked about holographic brain, does talk about a certain distributed aspect of memory through the brain. He would like to believe a sort of quantum mechanical superposition of these things is important in the formation of your thoughts. Now I think it is probably undoubtedly true that memory is in some sense distributed over large parts of the brain. Whether you need some quantum interference effects to bring these things together as is done in holography I would be rather doubtful about, but I don't think the brain is able to maintain these quantum superposition effects over large distances that would be required for the usual ideas of holography to apply. On the other hand it is probably true that memory is distributed through the brain so . . . if you are talking holography in the sense of a classically understandable combination of things from various regions, then I would say yes, memory is undoubtedly holographic or very likely holographic. If you are talking about something requiring a sophisticated quantum superposition as happens in optics, then my information would say no, that probably can't happen in the brain.

Do you think that we create our reality as we go?

Certainly to a large extent I think we do. What you expect to see and certainly your attitudes . . . I think everybody would agree, without being in any way mystical about it, that your intentions, attitudes, and beliefs about what is going to happen are all influencing what is going to happen. Whether there is a deeper hidden something going on, I'm not sure. I know people who do believe that and in my own life I've never had any thing that I would want to describe as coming from source like this, so I will maintain an open mind. Perhaps my own experience would incline me to skepticism, but certainly a lot of other people have a different belief about that.

Are you familiar with the movie, The Secret? It tells people they create whatever they think, so if they think a positive thing—for example, they want a new car—if they think about the car long enough, it eventually it appears. My personal opinion is that there is some truth to that—things can sometimes manifest somehow through thought—but I don't think we have complete free will to do that, because if we had complete free will, you could say, "Eva, I'm going to meet you at Starbucks at 3:00," and you may not get there at 3:00 because you don't have complete free will; something else is driving the car. So what do you think about the power of thought and the creation of mass in physical reality?

I suspect that insofar as you try to do controlled experiments to demonstrate this you will probably not be able to achieve it, and if it does exist it seems to be of a subtle sort of thing that doesn't function when you put it to a scientific test. I certainly know of people who tell me from their own experience that this works very well for them, and whether the reason that it works is their own attitudinal change or something actually in the physical world is something that certainly is difficult, if not impossible, to validate by scientific experiments. If it works for people then they should probably believe it.

Bill Tiller has done some work with fruit fly larvae where he actually shipped them to the other side of the country and placed intention through controlled circumstances that accelerated their growth rate by 25 percent—and they did that with just thought. How would quantum mechanics account for that? There are two batches, and one accelerated by 25 percent. He did the same with pH; he increased the pH in water by one point and decreased it by one point with only thought. How would that happen in quantum mechanics?

Some experimenters seem to be able to get effects like this and other experimenters don't, and of course there are a lot skeptical scientists who are very disinclined to believe something that can only be achieved by experimenters who believe it and it cannot be achieved by skeptics. The first question is, to what extent is it a real effect, and to what extent is it something else? I am not sure myself that it is a real effect, but if you want to suppose it is real quantum mechanics, it has both a virtue and a defect in that it is not complete; it is not dynamically or causally complete in its present form. There are certain causal gaps associated with what is called Process One, which is described as free choice on the part of the experimenter by Niels Bohr, for example, and Heisenberg, and some of the founders of quantum theory . . . so there are some aspects of quantum theory that are currently not closed. So, once you have an opening like that, if it turns out that some phenomena really does exist, there will be an opening in quantum theory to say, well, this thing that we don't yet understand can be understood . . . then you can do some development in the theory in such a way as to account for things like this. The fact that quantum theory is currently in an incomplete state does give it the capacity to perhaps explain things like this insofar as they really need to be explained.

Are you familiar with Robert Jahn's work?

Yes, quite.

Do you have any opinion on it?

As you probably know, they've been going for twenty years or more on their big experiment, and they developed an understanding of what works and what doesn't work. They devised a huge experiment that they were doing in conjunction with two laboratories in Germany, so all three were doing exactly the same protocol and with a massive database that would presume really subtle things. If things went in accord with how things had been going at this PEAR Institute up until then . . . well they did the experiment and the results were, no results in any of the three laboratories. And this was supposed to be a confirmation of twenty years of research at PEAR.

They did have results. I've talked to Brenda Dunne about this at length. They did have results.

The report that I hear is that results were negative in terms of what they expected. You can't in these experiments go after the fact and see things where you say "Oh, that wasn't in the original protocol, but now we see some strange things that we say is an effect." That doesn't count in science. In science you have got to say beforehand what you are expecting to see and what you are going to count as a positive result, and I think on that criteria, their results were no.

Basically what Brenda said was, they did ten thousand experiments where they placed intention that all the balls would fall to the left, and that's exactly what happened. Every ball fell to the left.

That's not the way I understand the data, and in particular we are talking now about these experiments that they did in these three laboratories independently. I've talked to people like Dean Radin and others who looked at it, and in terms of the stated goals of the experiment, which is the scientifically proper thing to use, the results were essentially no. So that's a big negative impact upon these claims. That doesn't mean that something is not going on but it is certainly a big negative.

I am floored at this perspective. What are your views about the idea of non-locality and entanglement at the macro level?

I certainly believe that there is non-locality in the world, and as far as the world conforms to the rules of quantum mechanics I do believe that you cannot explain the phenomena and explain the predictions of quantum theory if you disallow any sort of faster-than-light transmission of information. You are looking at macroscopic responses in your detecting devices, so the phenomena are totally macroscopic and yet . . . you can deduce just from the macroscopic phenomena the need for faster-than-light transmissions of information. It is true of course that there is a microscopic element, namely that the predictions were based on some theory involving individual photons. But certainly the phenomena are macroscopic and you don't have to say where the predictions came from. The predictions are predictions about macroscopic things, and just from the character of the macroscopic phenomena, there is enough to conclude that there is this non-local connectedness in the quantum universe that is non-understandable in terms of classical ideas.

Are you familiar with the work of Fritz Popp?

Yes I am.

What do you have to say about him basically stating that we are beings of light, and the more light one emits, the more consciously aware or evolved someone is?

Well, the work of Fritz Popp that I am familiar with has to do with the effect on biological systems of radiation. I think they are probably valid experiments, but I don't think they say that we are beings of light but rather that light has important influence on biological systems. To say that we are beings of light, I think, is far beyond what he would claim to have established. In fact I myself wrote a while ago in a book dedicated to David Bohm an article entitled, "Light at Foundations of Being," where in fact I was propounding something like this but certainly not in connection with anything that Fritz Popp was doing.

Somewhere I read that he had taken a corn stalk . . . .

Yes, that's right; corn is one of the things he worked with.

. . . and that what he saw with the equipment he had was an entire cornstalk of light, and the seedling literally grew into that stalk of light.

Perhaps that could be. Someone had a beam of light coming in from some direction, and the germination and the development of the corn was along the direction of the light. That wouldn't seem to be too unlikely, if it needs some sort sustenance like light beam—just like sunflowers.

What role do you see consciousness playing in non-locality and entanglement?

No one calls these experiments *explained* in quantum mechanics. Part of the proof, if you want to call it that, in non-locality, has to do with . . . you have to assume that it is one of the premises that the way the experiment is set up is, you have two regions, and you have an experimenter in each region who in principle performs one of two possible experiments—so you have altogether four partial combinations of experiments. You have to assume that choice made in each of the two regions between two possible experiments is a free choice. Somehow it could have gone either way, and you assume that it could go either way, and that no matter which way it goes the predictions at quantum theory will hold. The experimenter does one thing or he does the other. He sets up the situation so that one or another experiment is performed so there is in some ultimate sense not a freak in there. Nature apparently goes one way or the other. At least to us it appears to go one way or the other. So you do need—in order to even talk about this non-locality—to set the idea that there is some element of freedom here; free choice—and usually that is associated in orthodox quantum theory with the words that the experimenter can freely choose to do this or that. That is the usual connection; there is an element of freedom, which is granted to the experimenter in order to start talking about cause and effect. You want to be able to talk about changing a cause and seeing its effect in another. In order to start to talk about that way of understanding (cause and effect), you have to assume that the cause can be this or that. There are, of course, connections between freedom in some sense and volatility in the normal proof of non-locality.

What do you think this will mean for our understanding ten years from now? Does this—and if it does, how does it support the proof of the existence of God?

Right now I think we are probably in a transition period in terms of scientific understanding. At the moment the people in a materialistic universe would discount the importance of quantum theory. Understanding the role human beings in the universe . . . it's kind of strange, but many of the neuroscientists involved are still thoroughly wed to the idea that it can all be explained within the framework of classical mechanics, even though they all admit—and all the philosophers involved also admit—that they are all basically starting from classical concepts. There is just no way of understanding how consciousness comes out of this sort of understanding. There is no conceptual foundation in classical physics for the idea that something like thoughts should come out of brain activity, and they all admit that it is a huge mystery. In ten years I do believe the acceptance of a quantum mechanical view of nature will have made great strides, and people will realize that quantum mechanics provides a wonderful way of understanding a lot of data. So that is my answer to the first question.

Now on to the meaning of it all. All this progress in science, and yet we find no meaning in the universe. But once you go to really a thorough, complete quantum mechanical understanding, and the brain in particular and the human person in particular . . . then you see reasons and meaning, and you make a choice on the basis of what it means to you. You have reasons for doing what you do, instead of having this mechanical idea of human beings as mechanical devices like clocks that just tick along doing what they have been programmed to do. When that idea gets replaced by a quantum mechanical vision, where there is this element of freedom involved in which reasons and meaning can inject themselves into behavior or people and beings, it will be a huge difference. The whole moral, ethical theory is almost impossible in a mechanical view of the universe. The idea of *responsibility* makes no sense if everything was determined at the birth of a clocklike universe that's grinding its way to a pre-destined conclusion.

Quantum theory greatly changes the conception of how human beings fit into the universe. They are now able to fit in in a way that is able to allow them to inject meaning into the universe, and in accordance with the values that they have created their courses in life. That is what I see as the big important consequence of all this. The meaningfulness of human life is tremendously enhanced in that it creates a certain foundation for ethical behavior that is lacking in a mechanical universe.

I don't have an answer to the question about the existence of God. The meaning I was just talking about is on a local scale. I mean, individuals can have meaning and inject their local values into the behavior of their own bodies, first of all, and in the creation of societies built upon their values. That doesn't require the God-like overlord. It can say that values are important and meaning is important, but they develop on a more local scale without an overall objection aim. At the moment it seems to me that it's a more limited idea of human-based values and meanings we create in our own lives and try to implement.

There is the greater question—why are the laws of nature so friendly to the development of biological systems—and there is the same anthropic question of why that is true. There are laws to parameters in universe—charges and gravitational constants and many other parameters—that seem to just be finely tuned to permit life as we know it to evolve. So is that an accident? Then what sort of process caused those parameters to be what they are? Certainly a lot of scientists are debating this issue today. It is a quite a hot issue and so far we find they do not agree.

One answer according to some recent developments in string theory is that there should be, if you can think of this, a number this big: 10 to the power of 500 different possible universes in string theory. Now, if that many different universes exist, then it becomes not so unlikely that one exists that is friendly to life—and we are of course in one that is friendly to life—and the rest of them may be there, but without life. These questions are being batted around by scientists at the moment. Some are very unwilling to believe that we're all just living in a one-chance universe. In any case, there is no general agreement on how to answer. I'm not sure you need a God to specify that the laws will be such that it would be somewhat nicer from many points of view. I like to think that there may be a principle of favoring the evolution of complex systems, and such a universe that was designed in that way—favoring complexity—might account for the friendliness of the universe to live.

CHAPTER 7

Dr. Ervin Laszlo, Ph.D.

Ervin Laszlo is a systems philosopher, integral theorist, and classical pianist. Twice nominated for the Nobel Peace Prize, he has authored more than seventy books, which have been translated into nineteen languages, and has published in excess of 400 articles and research papers, including six volumes of piano recordings. Dr. Laszlo is generally recognized as the founder of systems philosophy and general evolution theory, and serves as the founder-director of the General Evolution Research Group and is a past president of the International Society for the Systems Sciences. He is also the recipient of the highest degree in philosophy and human sciences from the Sorbonne, the University of Paris, as well as of the coveted Artist Diploma of the Franz Liszt Academy of Budapest. Additional prizes and awards include four honorary doctorates. His appointments have included research grants at Yale and Princeton Universities, professorships for philosophy, systems sciences, and future sciences at the Universities of Houston, Portland State, and Indiana, as well as Northwestern University and the State University of New York. His career also included guest professorships at various universities in Europe and the Far East. In addition, he worked as program director for the United Nations Institute for Training and Research (UNITAR). In 1999 he was awarded an honorary doctorate by the Canadian International Institute of Advanced Studies in Systems Research and Cybernetics.

Eva: Dr. Ervin Laszlo and I are going to talk about one of his many books, Science and the Akashic Field, which is a wonderful book. Dr. Lazlo, you are an amazing man; you have been nominated for the Nobel Peace Prize two times already. Please tell us a little bit about yourself.

Dr. Lazlo: Eva, it is difficult to talk about yourself. It is the most difficult thing to know thyself. I have had a rather crazy life. I started out as a concert pianist—a child prodigy in Budapest, Hungary—and nobody ever thought that I would do anything else in my life but perform music. My mother was a piano teacher and my uncle, who lived in the same house, was a philosopher. So in the morning I did piano with my mother, and I would also go to school, and in the afternoon very often I would go for walks with my uncle who would share ideas and explain why it is important to inquire into what kind of world this is, and what our role is, etc. Then I thought all that was forgotten, and I was just going to go on as a pianist because I became very well-known as child as a concert pianist.

I don't really know what happened but I went on and played a lot of concerts all over the world, then I got married and settled down, and then I thought, well, let me think a little bit about more serious things. I got involved with some of the ideas that were coming to me in my childhood, and I decided to go into these ideas more seriously. I started reading and attending courses and ended up publishing a book more or less by chance. I then got invited to Yale University's philosophy department even though all I had was a music degree. Then I wrote more books and got a degree at the Sorbonne, in Paris, which was followed by various academic appointments. I ended up being on loan to the United Nations for a year, but stayed there seven years as Director of Research. Then I took a sabbatical at an old farmhouse in Italy and that sabbatical is still lasting. Since I left the United Nations I have been more busy than ever, but I'm now doing it when, where and how I want. So in a capsule form that is the past sixty years.

Did you do any training in quantum mechanics or physics or did you just "know"?

Not formally. I have many friends, and attended many courses; many at Yale University and also in Germany, and I inquired into the meaning of it all. Basically I was not concerned much with the mechanics—how to test it, how to make experiments, how to calculate it—I left that to people who already specialized in that area. My question was, "What does it mean?" I was trying to put together the results from different disciplines: physics, biology, cosmology, psychology, research. I could move very freely as a philosopher. I finally ended up teaching the philosophy of science. I had, so to speak, a license to move wherever I wanted.

What is your definition of consciousness? I have been conducting a little research project wherein I have been asking some of the luminaries in the world, what is that thing we call mind? You would be amazed at how many different answers I get for that one word.

That's certainly the biggest mystery of all. There seems to be two possibilities, if you want to be really consistent. Either our consciousness is all there is in the world because everything that appears to us appears to us through our consciousness. Either that is the totality of the world and everything is consciousness, or the world is really all physics and all matter—mass and energy—and consciousness is just the byproduct. I don't like either one of these solutions. I don't think either one is satisfactory. Here I use the word *satisfactory* in the sense that Alfred North Whitehead used it. He said a theory had to be not just correct, but also satisfactory, because of an inner sense which serves you well to determine whether you are on the right track or not.

Getting back to the definition, in answer to your question, I think consciousness is the inner read-out. It is what you get when you are part of the world, but you are seeing it from inside. You are seeing it from your own particular point of view. I believe that you see the whole world from your point of view because it is your consciousness, and I have mine. Each of us has this consciousness and it encompasses all the rest of the world from all points of view. I think that everything in the world has different levels of consciousness because each of us has, to use the modern term, read-out.

There is an external read-out and an internal read-out. The internal read-out is consciousness. The external read-out is our physics view and brain sciences—neurons and particles and molecules in the body. They are in everything in the whole universe and our consciousness is part of the consciousness of the cosmos.

Would it be subjective?

It is subjective but not in a negative sense. Everything is subjective in the sense that I am the subject. I experience the world. It is my consciousness. I feel it like this, and I'm pretty sure my dog feels the world also. I am pretty sure the plants feel the world. I think everything, even the cells in my body, feel the rest of the world in their own way, at their own level of organization and complexity. We can feel it in a very articulate way because our brain is highly complex and allows us to articulate the cosmic consciousness, which is in the universe in a way in which we can see many more things. We can identify things and we can think about them. We have a highly evolved kind of consciousness because we are highly evolved organisms.

In your view, would consciousness also consist of sensate awareness, emotional awareness, cognitive awareness, and self-awareness?

In a general sense I use consciousness as everything that you feel; that happens to you . . . everything that you perceive. That means all intuitions also. I am not using only the sense of self perception . . . that's part of it, but whatever happens to you, whatever you intuit, whatever goes on with you as living and experiencing reality, is part of this dream that accompanies you from birth to death. I think we write another theme that I am pretty sure continues after physical death as well. This is consciousness, the totality of all the things one experiences.

Do you think the irreducible unit would be the totality of everything?

Everything consists of the whole, but you cannot take the whole apart and you cannot know everything all at once.

Whitehead—who is one of the great influences on me—said everything is connected with everything else we would logically obliged to say everything is one. But you can't say everything is one and it would make sense. So we have to take things apart. There is irreducibility to everything, but in order to know things and see things, we are analyzing them to pieces, and it is challenging to put it together. We need to see the forest even though what we see in front of us are trees.

What would your definition of mind be?

I don't see anything we could call mind. It is different if you say consciousness is limited to conscious awareness. Yes. If you think of consciousness as meager specific conscious awareness of yourself, or of your world, or of your perception, then of course mind is much more encompassing. But if you use consciousness as the totality of all of your experience then it is equal to mind. Your mind is consciousness. Consciousness is the mind.

I am asking these specific kinds of questions because it is my goal to help bridge the gap between science and spirituality.

Yes, I appreciate and support that.

So many classical scientists and allopathic medical doctors don't understand that it doesn't boil down to the organ we know as the brain. I am trying to create an understanding that consciousness is different from the brain, and consciousness is different from what they see the mind to be because they think that mind is contained within brain. Do you think that the brain thinks or do you think it is an organ that processes consciousness, that brain mediates consciousness or mediates awareness?

I think the great tie-in is between science and spirituality. If you look at the world, the universe itself is intelligent in some sense. There are big arguments in that too, which we can get onto later if you like, but there are good reasons to believe that this is not an accidental world. Too many things are fine tuned in such a way that certain things can happen. If you think that the universe has governing consciousness, then the tie-in with spirituality is to say that our brain is part of this world. We know it is connected to this world in multiple ways. In more and more ways we are discovering that the way the brain picks up the rest of the world is the way it extracts from this universe of consciousness, and that particular segment is my consciousness. It is the individual consciousness.

We are simply articulating the totality, the total sea of consciousness which is there in the cosmos, into our individual consciousness, and it would be a big mistake to think that the rest doesn't exist—that that is all there is. It would be a big mistake also to think that this consciousness that I have is merely just a byproduct by the great self operating inside one's skull. So I think there is a direct tie-in because all the great spiritual traditions talk about an initial cosmos, oneness, or energy that bursts forth, and is descending, and gradually becoming more and more material until it becomes the body—and consciousness is something that is associated with that. You have symbolic ways of phrasing it; science phrases it in a different way, but it comes to the same thing. We are not separate from the rest and we are not purely material. We are not purely just mind either; we have both aspects. We have an external aspect which, if you look at from the outside, it appears to you as a physical organism or physical-biological-chemical organism . . . and if you look at it from the inside—from the point of your own experience—then this same organism appears to you as mind; as the totality of the flow of consciousness.

What do you believe to be the source of creativity and intentionality?

Because we are part of a conscious, intentional, and self-evolving universe, the tremendous drive in nature—the growth, force, and complex system that we call living—is a fantastic act of constant creativity. Occasional tremendous breakthroughs, like when bacteria learn to photosynthesize or learn to feed on oxygen, and then to feed on sunshine, and then to become multi-cellular instead of just staying a single cell. The multi-cell begins to mutate in such a way that they can live in a complex environment and contain more and more structure and information to use and govern themselves increasingly. All that is a constant act of creativity called the creative advance into novelty. Always something new is happening and the entire universe is moving constantly into novelty. From the big bang on through the galaxy and the play-out of the tremendous symphony of galactic evolution— star systems, planets—to forms of life that have evolved. So that is constant creativity and the part of that tremendous symphony is a drive towards structure and complexity.

How do you think the original intention began? Obviously it came from energy . . . how do you think that original intention or thought of creativity began?

In the universe or in the individual?

In the universe. I can see a field out there but how did it get started?

That's the million-dollar question. It's the biggest mystery of all how it got started. There are various ways of looking at, it but you said it is all energy. I think here right away we have to add a term. I think the basis of the universe is both energy and information. Information is what structures. Energy is all there is. There is no such thing as matter. This may come as a shock to many people but matter is finely structured energy. There are standing waves of energy; we know that very well. Particles are really not material, they are swirls of energy. They maintain themselves in the same place although they are interconnected and they are very mysterious beasts but they are certainly not just bits of matter. Everything else is made of particles, atoms, cells, crystals, and so on. There is no matter but that doesn't matter so to speak because matter is energy—which is the hardware of the universe. What there is, is various forms of energy, but how this energy behaves is not accidental, and it was there from the very beginning, and it gives the laws of nature. There are laws of nature. There are ways energy can behave, ways the particles can combine with each other and the ways energy can be radiated through electromagnetism, gravitation, nuclear fields, or other ways that we haven't yet discovered. All of this depends on information. The way this universe is, is the information that was there from the very beginning which is structuring, governing and evolving energy.

"Physics people" tend to have a problem with the word "frequency," but I don't know any other way to describe what I am trying to ask. How do you think the source of intentionality or creativity conveys the information to an individual? Do you think it goes through electromagnetism, pulsing, and/or voltage? Like the Morse code with some kind of voltage behind it?

The question makes perfect sense it is a very good and important question. Here is where I can refer to the theories that I have been developing in the past fifteen-twenty years. I have been looking at evolution as a series of interconnected systems that moves towards more and more complexity and meaning, but how does this communicate with one another. Here is where I say that information is coming to us in multiple ways but it is not accidental and is not limited to what the established sciences recognize as electromagnetic information, gravitational information, or nuclear information.

I think that there is an information field in itself. Information is structured and is there; whatever you do produces information, and this information is registered. This is a different kind of concept, but a concept that follows very logically from all of our experiences. Nothing happens purely by chance. Nothing happens purely as an individual thing that is not connected with other things, and when something happens once it is conserved. It is there, it influences whatever happens after that so nothing is purely evanescent. Nothing disappears or vanishes without a trace. This is what I call the Akashic Field or the field similar to what the Hindus sages have called the Akasha—the fundamental medium of the universe that records everything.

I think what comes to us is coming to us through intuition; through information of the conscious but also through subconscious. Very often we have feelings, we sense certain things and those things are perfectly good legitimate sources of information . . . sometimes produced by our brain alone, inside, and there is no particular reference to outside. But many times, in fact most of the time, there is something in the world that is communicated to us not always through the so called senses—feeling, seeing, hard or soft, hearing and smelling things—but coming to us in our subconscious, and then it is a question for us to become conscious of it.

Our brain is an instrument of very high fine-tuning. You mentioned frequency before. The brain can pick up a very high and wide range of frequencies in the world, and our conscious awareness, especially in the western world, filters out a lot of things because we don't believe that they exist, so our conscious awareness only contains a very small fragment of all that actually reaches the brain. The brain is a receiver and a transmitter at the same time; it is a transceiver. What the brain receives, we only become aware normally of a very small fragment.

How do you think that individuality exists? Do you think the soul is in our aura, our electromagnetic field? How does individuality arise?

Again we are at the very edge of what is knowable or what is known for the time being, but I think we can get further still. There are a lot more things that are knowable than we know to date. Certainly each thing in this universe has individuality. What I mean by that is, the individual particles ranging from the cell of the organism, all the way out to the stellar systems, galaxies, and entire solar systems, all have individuality.

Let me use an analogy like a wave. You look at a wave and then you see that the wave as having an individuality. It's traveling. Maybe when it hits the shore it breaks; but as long as it's on the body of water, a wave can travel. There are certain kinds of waves that are known as solitrons. They are very curious waves; they look like they were actually sort of balls moving around on top of a surface of a liquid or some kind of a medium. They look like they are individual, but actually they are part of that medium. They are just a very complex kind of wave. I look at particles and all things that have individuality as a kind of complex wave traveling over the entire sea: which is the sea . . . which is space-time . . . which is the entire universe as an interconnected whole—a constant underlying whole. It is a field. Individuality is there as a wave traveling over a complex sea. I know that is not an easy definition but it is the best I can do.

Do you think it literally has something to do with the body and the aura? Do you think the body helps establish individuality?

We are bodies in the sense of what I call the external read-out. We are more than just the body because when we sense the world, we sense the world not *as* a body, we sense it *through* our body—but we sense it as a mind. It comes to us as our consciousness. Individuality is a body/mind individuality. It is there and it is constant. What I am trying to emphasize is that it is not separate . . . and here is another breach we have with spirituality. In spirituality you know that we are one. We are part of a much larger whole and if you consider this newer approach from the new science, you will see that the individual body is a complex wave, very much part of the whole. It is just an illusion that we are separate.

That was a really good way to describe it for someone who doesn't understand. Thank you. Do you think we have complete free will? What I mean by this is I am a believer of non-duality, and I think that we are not driving the car. If we had complete free will then you could say, "Eva meet me at the store at 3:00," and we would both be there at 3:00; not one minute before and not one minute after. We can't guarantee that, so I don't think we have complete free will.

There is no complete free will and there is no complete determinism either. I think that what you can see is how the freedom is built into the universe. I don't think the future is decided. It is not decided by the past or the present. It is always a creative advance into the next step. It is a question of degree. The more complex an organism, or an entity of any kind—could be a society or an information system—the more complex it is; the more it internalizes the factors that render it free. The decisions come more from the inside of the system rather than from the outside. Look at a very simple thing like a piece of matter of some kind like a piece of iodine or stone it happens from the outside. It doesn't decide what happens to it. Quanta, through particles, have an element of self-decision . . . but when you get to complex systems they more and more decide what is happening to them. They have a degree of freedom that increases with the complexity of decision-making possibilities, like a complex computer can make many more decisions than a simple mechanical typewriter. A mechanical typewriter carries out what you bang out on the keyboard. A complex computer gets signals and its program decides what it is going to do.

Do you think there is a quantum of self, a quantum of time, and a quantum of consciousness such as the consciousness unit?

There are individual units that we can break down, but I think they are fairly artificial. There is a great debate that has been going on in the physics community now ever since Einstein came up with the Theory of Relativity almost one hundred years ago, but particularly since the quantum evolution in the 19th Century, the debate continues: are there quanti? I think the great challenge is to see the continuity beyond the quanta; the individual bits and pieces. It turns out that everything that can be measured is constant quanta; constant, separate chunks. These chunks are also part of something deeper; so in my mind, once we break things apart, units exist. For example time is a continuous flow but we take it apart into seconds, minutes, hours, and so on. Things in front of us are continuous waves, but a continuous medium—something like ocean waves—generally appears to us as individual waves. Sometimes we make the mistake—very often, in fact—of thinking of the waves as being individual, and forgetting that they are actually waves of, or waves *in*, something much larger than themselves.

I see the universe as being infinite and continuing and with a hierarchy that goes up to a peak and then maybe inverts and starts over and continues constantly. Does that make sense?

A lot of sense indeed. But there is an ancient notion—again talking about bridges between religion and science—the ancient notion in the Hindu philosophy has always been that universes come and go to evolve. The cosmos breathes in and out. When it exhales the power force can move forward and develop and evolve. When it breathes in they come back again to the source, and then in the next breath another universe continues.

The new concept in cosmology is that there are multiverses. The universe is not all there is, this universe is part of a series of a cycle of universes sometimes called the megaverse. The fact is that there are cycles of universes. Each universe evolves up to a maximum point; then, as we know from all the physical processes we can observe in the cosmos, it can't continue forever. At a given time the kind of processes that build matter—particles into systems and eventually into galaxies—must stop because the energy gets used up. This universe then starts to collapse, and the last of this enormous galaxy *records* collapses . . . then everything that has been there—that has manifested—disappears. But the Akashic Records retain all this information. Then other universes can burst forth from the void—the most fundamental element from which all things emerge—and possibly burst forth even before one universe disappears, because some records will provide the beginnings of other universes. So absolutely what you say is absolutely right. There are series of cycles, which involve everything there is.

How do you know these things, Ervin? Did you have a spiritual epiphany or was it just a gradual process?

It has resulted from a lot of inquiry, but you have to *know*, so to speak, what you are looking for. That is the biggest question. You get flooded by data if you just try to pick up everything you know, everything that is around you. You can't get much further than a single small part of a single discipline because there is so much knowledge in every one of the disciplines. One lifetime is not enough to pick it all up. You have to know what is really significant and how then to put it together. If I can contribute something, or have contributed something, it is the result of the ability to pick out things that I believe are significant; that reflect something, that present good reasons to consider them "reality," and put them together so they make some kind of sense—not arbitrary or subjective items, but those that offer us good reason to believe that they reflect something that is really happening in the world.

There were epiphanies, by the way. I had several cases like that and they provide sudden insights and you can follow them up. Looking for an Akashic Field, for example, was the result of an epiphany. Then there was the question of following it up.

I'd like to share something that happened to me because it changed my life. I was a fundamental Baptist walking around in the world; then I had some kind of horrible dark night of the soul and then something happened in my sleep where I thought I went to the other side and saw my dead father. The next morning I woke up and I knew about all of the stuff that I am asking you and I had never heard of it before. What causes that to happen? How does that happen?

I know this happens and I had a similar experience wherein I knew things all of a sudden. One has intuitions, which usually come at the borderline between sleep and wakefulness; when one is not in deep sleep, but when one allows the brain to pick up information that normally is suppressed. I see that information comes as a very small fragment when one is conscious. In the state of light dreaming, or being semi-conscious, much more information can come. If one is lucky enough and remembers some of it, takes it seriously, and uses it, great benefit can result.

This is one of the reasons why I have started investigating some fifteen years ago this possibility that information is there in the world and available; it's a question of digging it up. That's why I started talking about an information field, which I now call the Akashic Field or the A-Field. I think you were connected into the A-Field—actually you are all the time connected to the A-Field, but you became conscious of this connection—and actually picked up things from there. Then you woke up and some of this information that came to you informed you and suffused in your mind, becoming very fertile . . . and changed your life.

What do you think the connection is with having some kind of horrible dark night of the soul? Almost every luminary I have talked to who has had such an epiphany has had some kind of awful dark night of the soul just prior to the event.

One of the principles regarding any kind of creativity or building something new is, you always have to overcome the resistance of the old. You have to forget. There is a very nice saying by a great physicist, Werner Heisenberg, who said the problem is not that we can't learn but that we can't forget. We have difficulty forgetting the old. The dark night of the soul is a way of forgetting what we had learned before; liberating ourselves from the crypt of habitual ways of thinking and looking at the world. It is waking up to the fact that there is something else. The force of habit is the greatest block to creativity and to learning. To learn something new . . . sometimes you have to get a shock. I didn't have this kind of dark night of the soul, partly because my life has always been so unconventional that I have never had a routine life. My life just happened the way it did.

Lucky you!

I didn't even go to school regularly until I was fifteen. I got my degrees, but I did it in my own way.

I would like to talk about the B flat sound that I hear in my head. Every person I've interviewed who was extremely consciously awake hears that sound as well.

There are two things. One is the subjective feeling of it; the other thing is to find an explanation for it. The subjective feeling seems to be pretty widespread if you are sensitive to sounds. If you are not, you can hear anything and it doesn't mean much. But if you are sensitive to sounds then the B flat is very comforting. It is very much like a home base. The B flat is something which seems to be the home base for all things. Everything can be built from there and returns to there. That is the subjective sensation.

The actual explanation is that there are the frequencies of the pressure waves that are traveling in the cosmos that are being caused by the collapse of entire galactic cores corresponds to a basic frequency 80 octaves deeper than the audible range of B flat. It is one of the subtonics of the B flat that you hear. There is something in the universe which gives you this frequency, which is the most basic kind of pressure waves or waves traversing the cosmic field altogether.

It seems since that B flat would be the frequency upon which the original intention was placed. If someone hears that sound in their head, and they were to meditate or place intention on that sound, it seems to me like it would manifest quicker.

People probably respond to that. It is more like a connecting sound. It helps us establish the contact. Let me add something, which I think is simple to recognize: we are all the time connected. It's like being connected to the internet all the time. The reason people don't recognize it is because they don't click the "get message" button on their email system or URL to pick up a website. We are always connected but just not aware. B flat is a basic tone, and if we become conscious of it, it helps us press the right button. It helps us fine-tune our brain so it picks up the signals of information. Another analogy would be the antennae. The B flat helps us to orient our antennae so we can pick up more information in such a way that we can become aware of it, because it is there all the time; we are just not aware of it.

That is so interesting to me. Do you think that the Zero Point Field—not the entire field, but the edge of it—would be the dividing line between duality, possibly? On that side there is just pure potential and black darkness, no stars or light . . . and on this side there are stars, light, and physical mass.

What is technically called the Zero Point Field is the most significant part because I think it seems to be electromagnetic, but it is a technicality. There is something which underlies all the manifest forms of energy, matter, and mass, but as I've said matter is really a form of energy. This underlying thing is a field—the most basic field that there is—and really contains everything. Out of this spring the different particles—positive and negative charged particles; matter and anti-matter—and these make up the known universe. There is no real duality except that everything that comes forth from it always had a positive and negative charge; a yin and a yang. This is what gives its design. It's all there, it all comes from the field because the field is energy and information together.

Do you know anything about magnetic monopoles?

Yes.

What I would like to know is, if you think a thought, there has to be some way that makes things create things in our life . . . good feelings and bad feelings, the sensate things. I wonder if magnetic monopoles would be that thing where, when you think a thought, it causes the energy to transmit and receive at the same time, being possibly why what goes around comes around? If you think a thought and it had a positive charge then it would transmit and receive a positive charge. Maybe that would be what manifested tomorrow and the next day. If someone thinks negatively all of the time and the thought transmits and receives a negative charge, then that might be why they constantly negative things happening in their life. Possibly by being in the moment, not transmitting that negative charge you could possibly turn your life around. Do you think that has anything to do with magnetic monopoles?

It is a good analogy. It is a good way of trying to come to grips with the phenomena that certain kinds of things affect all kinds of things. I think there is an explanation which comes closer to what is likely to be in reality, and that is to think in terms of holograms. Holograms are very, very complex patterns, and the hologram is a very curious thing. It has all the information that is contained in the whole, in every little part of all there is. The whole picture is in a hologram, and if you illuminate any part of it all of it is there.

But what is more curious about a hologram is that there are a whole lot of different holograms with all different kinds of patterns in a complex holographic field or holographic medium. One hologram will attach itself or start to communicate immediately with compatible holograms which have the same frequency. The hologram chooses. Like chooses like. A hologram chooses its counterparts, its communicators. I think the same happens with thought. Certain kinds of thought processes will choose the corresponding kind of processes which are there in the field, which are communicated by other people, so they put you in touch with different kinds of things. I think that process happens continuously, although this seems to be taking it very far, but I think it continues also between lifetimes, probably your kind of thinking, psyche, soul, or whatever you want to call it. I call this the informational bundle that is your consciousness. It continues to attract that kind of other phenomena so that when you are reborn, you have sequential information bundles that correspond to the idea of karma. It corresponds to the kind of thinking, intentions, or mentality that you have developed in your present lifetime.

Interesting. Do you think that would have anything to do with quantum condensates?

There are a lot of theories, all having their own particular origin. It is difficult to apply them beyond a given range but there are quantum phenomena. The important thing is to see the context within which this phenomenon takes place. We are all condensates. We are macroscopic quantum systems ourselves, and the brain operates in that way. Certainly it would be a big mistake to think that quantum phenomena only apply to the very, very small quanta or mini particles. They apply to living systems; brain and the mind of consciousness operate in a quantum domain. It picks up information, it sends information, and it simultaneously relates a lot of different facts.

Is there anything you would like to discuss that I have not already asked you?

I would like to get a little more down to earth, so to speak, and say why this kind of new insight that we have been talking about is so important today. The crisis that we are facing is basically a crisis of understanding; a crisis of incoherence and breakdown in communication. It is a crisis because a person doesn't understand others, doesn't understand nature, and cannot relate to the world around them . . . resting on this mistaken belief that our consciousness is just something produced inside the skull that simply depends on the brain, and our brains are separate from mind, and we can only best communicate if we talk to each other. The idea that we have a deeper connection gets suppressed and is not recognized. This leads to a lot of loss of meaning. It leads people to believe that we are separate from everything else.

I would like to quote the great psychologist William James, who said in one of the last things that he wrote, which was a reflection about what he had learned in his many years of investigating the psyche. He said that finally we are like islands in the sea, separate at the surface but connected in the deep underneath. To recover this kind of connection with each other is fundamental to recovering meaning and the kind of understanding that we need to get along in the world with each other without competing and killing and marginalizing each other. In this complex world we need much more understanding and this understanding will come much faster if we open our minds and our brain and become a receiver of all the important subtle signals and information that we get from the world around us. Press the button that says "get message" and receive it.

CHAPTER 8

Rollin McCraty, Ph.D.

Rollin McCraty has been with the Institute of HeartMath since its inception in 1991. He worked with founder Doc Childre to formulate the organization's research goals and create its Scientific Advisory Board. Dr. McCraty is a Fellow of the American Institute of Stress, holds memberships with the International Neurocardiology Network, American Autonomic Society, Pavlovian Society, and Association for Applied Psychophysiology and Biofeedback, and is an adjunct professor at Claremont Graduate University. He and his research team regularly participate in collaborative studies with other U.S. and international scientific, medical, and educational institutions. Dr. McCraty is an internationally recognized authority on heart-rate variability, heart-rhythm coherence, and the effects of positive and negative emotions on human psychophysiology. He is widely published in those and other research areas.

Eva: Please tell us a little about HeartMath before we get started.

Rollin: Our mission at the HeartMath Institute is to help establish heart-based living and global coherence by inspiring people to connect with the intelligence and guidance of their own heart. The research center is really about researching the physiology of the human spirit—not in a religious or woo-woo kind of way, but with very rigorous hard-core science.

Rollin McCraty, Ph.D.

What do you mean by coherence?

That's not an easy one to answer but let me give you the definitions that make up what we mean by coherence, because there are several. The first definition in a dictionary would cite someone trying to be logical and coherent in a conversation or argument; coherent speech. In physics it means when multiple systems synchronize and work at a much higher level of efficiency. So we mean it in both of those ways. What we have found is that it is really our emotional systems that drive coherence in our bodies, or not. Negative emotions drive us into incoherence, meaning our nervous system doesn't communicate to different parts of the body . . . kind of like driving the car with one foot on the brake and the other on the accelerator at the same time. Conversely, positive emotions renew energy instead of draining, and drive the system into more harmonious interactions. At the energetic level there is also a type of coherence going on as well.

Does this have anything to do with the autonomic nervous system?

Sure. The autonomic nervous system is one of the primary systems . . . it is a very high-level system in the hierarchy of control within the body systems that ultimately controls the immune system and the hormonal system to a large degree. The autonomic nervous system is a main communication pathway within the body that allows our thoughts and emotions to interact with the body.

Please tell us about the Global Coherence Project. What you are doing, who you are doing it with, and what does it mean to mankind?

The Global Coherence Monitoring System is part of a the Global Coherence Initiative , which is much wider in its scope as a global network of sensitive magnetic field detectors that are specifically designed to monitor fluctuations in the earth's geomagnetic field—but more importantly, excitations, pulsations, and resonances in the earth's ionosphere.

What is the purpose of wanting to know this information?

Great question! That's going to take me a little while to fully answer because there are multiple reasons. First let me tell you that one of our partners on this is a fairly famous theoretical physicist named Dr. Elizabeth Rauscher. She's the one who really first started looking at the ionosphere in a more rigorous way, and that changes in these resonances can occur and Elizabeth first found was that about two weeks prior to an earthquake or volcanic eruption, a signature shows up in the earth's field.

How does it show up?

It shows up in changes in certain frequencies that occur.

Are they measureable?

Yes . . . with these sensors that I am describing.

You can tell in which area there will be an occurrence?

Yes, more or less. To give you an example . . . through the 1980s Dr. Rauscher accurately predicted the eruption of Mt. St. Helens in Washington, but in the year and one-half following that, they had 84% percent accuracy in all the seismic activity in a one hundred square mile area around that single detector.

There are different levels in the ionosphere. I've come to think of these things like the membranes around cells. These layers protect us; they hold the atmosphere in, and protect the earth from the cosmic radiation and heavy protons from the sun; these types of things. Think of them kind of like soap bubbles and each layer has a different consistency because they are each made of different charged ions. Different plasmas each one with its own resonant frequency. Imagine a soap bubble floating through the air, and you poked on it; that would create waves that go around that bubble. You can think of the ionosphere like that. When the space shuttle takes off and goes up through the different layers, it pokes holes through the layers as it goes through them and this creates resonances that resonate around the entire planet. She was able to see in these detectors where the space shuttle is at as it goes through different layers because of the oscillation patterns. Knowing that, we know the frequency that is associated with each layer. Make sense so far?

Yes. Could give us some idea of the frequency ranges?

Mainly they are between zero and 500 hertz, so fairly low-frequency stuff. There is a main kind of frequency around 7.8 hertz, and what interests most people is the lower regions, because they are the same as human rhythms. That's a great question, actually.

A fair amount of work has been done already looking at correlations between changes in these resonances in the ionosphere, mostly driven by solar activity, solar flares that shoot out heavy protons that hit the ionosphere and create a type of incoherence in the ionosphere. There is a lot of activity. Those changes in the earth's magnetic field have already been associated with things like changes in brainwaves, nervous system activity on a mass level, performance in sports tasks and our ability to remember things. A lot of work has been done in energetic sensitivity, ESP experiments which are also affected. Also, the ability of plants and algae to uptake and synthesize the nutrition they need are directly affected by the earth's field.

When we come to the humans, when the earth's field is in a more incoherent state there are more traffic accidents, and more tickets are written for traffic violations. A very large study has been done where you can historically that a strong correlation between heart attacks and strokes when there are solar flares which cause changes in the earth's field. An increase in depression and suicide rates which are also correlated with solar flares and changes in the earth's field.

What frequency would that fall in, do they know?

I don't think they really know the frequency going on in the earth's field yet. That is the kind of thing we will be able to do with the new system we are developing. That is one of the things we will be able to look at when we get the global network set up.

Now what is really interesting is, in terms of the human system is that changes in geomagnetic conditions, most affect the rhythm of the human heart, or heart rate variability which you know one of the areas we are fairly well known for.

What does it do?

It changes the amount of variability that people have in their beat to beat hear rate. A healthy person's heart rate changes with every single heartbeat. That's fairly new for a lot of people to know, because not so long ago it was thought that a sign of good health was a steady heart rhythm. In other words, if a single heartbeat equates to 70 beats per minute, you would think that the next one would be near that 71 or 70—something like that—unless some exercise was done to get the heart rate up. It's exactly the opposite of that. Our rates are always varying beat to beat and it's quite surprising how much variability is going on. We now know that a loss of this variability is one of the best predictors of future fairly serious health problems, including sudden cardiac death.

When the heart rate variability changes, does it also change what is going on within cells?

Probably. This is a little bit off our topic, but most of us looking at heart rate rhythms are coming to look at it like it is a global indicator of your vitality, your well-being, as a system; as a whole. It is a very important fundamental rhythm. Lower variability than it should be for our age is correlated with "not good things," let's put it that way. In cardiology it is used to predict an eightfold increased risk of sudden cardiac death, arrhythmias and things like that. It is also correlated with cancer and all causes of mortality, which is a very important finding. It's really showing that the autonomic nervous system is primarily affected in the communication between the heart and the brain, or the source of heart rate variability.

Back to your project, how are you going to get these machines out there? Do you need people do that?

We will, but right now we're developing the infrastructure; how these sensors are going to talk back to the central lab, that type of thing.

Rollin McCraty, Ph.D.

I saw an announcement once that said you need volunteers or people to help. What can someone help do?

At this point we really need to get the project funded, so that would be one way that people could certainly help. On the technology side we've got a pretty good team already in place. We've got a site here that we're testing and we've been monitoring changes in the earth's field around the clock for a while now. The next step is to get several remote sites up and running so we can do triangulation experiments and that type of thing.

Do you have any feedback yet from the information that you have?

We certainly know that the new designs of the sensors are working very well and that we are able measure all of the frequencies. The next step is getting a global network of them installed. We estimate that it will take around twelve sensing stations around the globe to do that.

Have you talked to any of the U.S. officials? Are they open to this or interested?

I haven't a clue and no we haven't spoken to any government officials.

Can you measure mass consciousness and individual consciousness?

Not necessarily individually. That's where I was going next; good question. I was talking about the work that has already been done. We already know that changes in the earth's field affect humans on a mass scale—increased heart attacks, heart rhythms, and that type of thing. We are living within—embedded within— the earth's magnetic field. It's really not that difficult to conceive that we would be affected by modulations in these complex fields. So that is not that far reaching. But it's a much more far-reaching proposition to suggest that the earth's field can be influenced or modulated by *human emotions,* and that is exactly what we are suggesting, and it's our main reason for developing this global system. That's why we call it the global coherence monitoring system.

163

When a global event evokes a negative response, you can think of that as producing a planetary stress wave.

Like when 9/11 happened and everyone got depressed?

Exactly; there is great data on this, and that is exactly what happened. There was truly a planetary stress wave. I can describe some of that data to you a little bit later if you like. But conversely what we are proposing here is that a mass positive emotional response can create a global coherence wave, and if we get enough people to personal coherence at the same time with the same intention, we can start *offsetting* the global stress waves.

Dean Radin and I had a conversation about this kind of mass intention, and he said, if you had a pond with a thousand people around it, and each person had a pebble that they threw randomly, you would get a bunch of little splashes in the pond. But if everyone threw a pebble of the same size, with the same force, at exactly the same time to the millisecond, all the water would come out. Will it matter how the intention is placed? Do we have to have a very sharply focused intention, or can we just think good things?

From my way of thinking, and what our research shows is that thinking is not going to have that much of an impact. It is really emotionality. It is really the feelings that we carry or that we are feeling that create the much stronger waves. I think of emotional feelings as generating a literal wave that interact with the magnetic systems. There is evidence for this but it is a whole other topic. We've been able to show that you can measure one person's heartbeat and another person's brain wave quite a few feet away so our nervous systems are exclusively sensitive at detecting these emotional fields that ride on the heartbeat.

Do you know about Bill Tiller's discovery about magnetic monopoles?

I know about his theory.

Would what happened possibly have something to do with magnetic monopoles?

It is certainly possible.

Could you tell us how that might play together?

I think that would be a better question for Bill in terms of a magnetic monopole but I can certainly say that magnetic fields, whether there are monopoles or not, seem to be a key to so many things in terms of mediating the kinds of effects we are talking about here.

How would this relate with the Schumann Resonance?

The Schumann Resonance – a German physicist, Schumann, was the first to propose and measure suggested there were oscillations in the earth's atmosphere.

There is an individual human consciousness we know that; we have our individuality, and then the mass consciousness. Would you suspect that the individual consciousness would be at a higher resonance or a lower resonance than the mass consciousness?

I don't quite understand the question.

If the human individual consciousness has to resonate at some frequency between some range to exist, that would be at one place. The mass consciousness has to vibrate at a different level or else it would be the same as the individual consciousness. Would mass consciousness resonate higher or lower than individual consciousness.

Ok I think I get what you are saying. Here's another way of thinking about that. What you would call the standard background consciousness/awareness level which here at Heartmath we call 3-D consciousness. That is the average of the mass consciousness. Of course there are individuals who have more awareness than others so they would be on the far right of the bell curve so to speak, which would have a higher vibration rate, certainly with an increased awareness level.

The resonance of a more aware individual would be at a higher rate than the mass consciousness; a higher frequency.

Yes, exactly. And what the planetary shift that we are intending to facilitate is really all about is moving the baseline of the mass consciousness to an increased level of awareness or a higher consciousness.

How do we go about facilitating that so that everyone participates?

There are a number of ways, not just one. The Global Coherence Project we are describing here is one of those ways of being able to measure and show that when groups of people get into individual coherence, we can measure that with devices like the emWave which used to be called the Freeze Framer that measures your heart rhythm coherence. We are proposing that when people do these mass-type experiments, if they get into individual coherence first, then they can think up and have far more effectiveness than if we are just all off doing our different kinds of things. When doing this we are not really at the individual coherence level.

What else would you like to share with us that I haven't thought to ask?

Not only are we affected *by* the field, we also have an effect *on* the field. You mentioned you had already spoken with Dean Radin so I know you are aware of the Global Consciousness Project he's involved with, which is in some ways a similar concept to what we are talking about here. They have a network of random number generators around the globe. What they are measuring doesn't work very well with an individual, but when you get large groups of people having a common emotional experience, the random number generator stops being as random. 9/11 is a great example of that for it is some of the strongest data yet on it.

Please elaborate for those who don't know what we are talking about.

A random number generator is basically an electronic device that spews out random noise, kind of like white noise. If you had an old TV with the white background snow turned on, and suddenly you had an emotional response, some type of pattern would show up on the screen. That is kind of what is happening with the random event generator; it stops being random. A pattern has now been introduced.

In my own way of thinking, basically there are these electronic devices which are transistor or diode junctions, which are ultimately right at the interface with what people like to call the quantum domain where we can measure, so if there is a type of coherence introduced into the quantum level, it bleeds over into the electronic devices, and they stop being random. On 9/11 there was a huge effect, but what is important, it was not in just a single detector, like in New York; the effect was in *all* the random number generators around the entire globe. So that's why we can say a global stress wave occurred. What is truly amazing in this case is, the point where they stopped being random started occurring about four hours *before* the first attack. So it also shows a mass intuition—the intuition of a lot of people. They woke up that morning and something was off, but they just didn't know what it was.

The random event generators can't tell where it is going to happen though, can they?

No. They just respond to large emotion.

With your new equipment will you be able to tell where something is going to happen?

We think we will in terms of earthquakes and that type of thing . . . don't know yet.

It will be interesting to see if some major event occurs if your machine gets coherence in the area where it is going to happen.

This is a little different. What we are proposing here is not measuring the output of random number generators, but actually directly measuring the earth's magnetic field. As it turns out there are two satellites that are designed to measure space weather that are in geo-synch orbit. They are 24,000 miles out in space and there is one on each side of the United States. One of sensors on them is a magnetic field detector and you can see what looks like a circadian rhythm, like a sine wave like pattern, over a twenty-four hour period. If you look at the five or six days coming up to 9/11 there is a nice sine wave pattern and right at the time of the 9/11 attack there is a huge spike and a very incoherent pattern starting to emerge in the earth's magnetic field.

Is this just before the occurrence or while it was happening?

Good question and we are not really sure until we get a little bit better data. This is after the fact and we can only get a certain resolution, so I can't really answer that yet. Trying to get the raw data is one of the things we are working on now. What you see is, the days after 9/11 in the earth's field is very incoherent erratic all over the place. There is actually some pretty good evidence. Measurement of one thing like this doesn't prove anything but it's amazing, the correlation that was seen here.

Have you spoken with Henry Stapp about this?

I haven't.

He acknowledges that something very miniscule happened with Bob Jahn's work and the random event generators, but he doesn't think that it tells us anything. He seems to think that it is random and nonmeaningful, and I don't understand how he can think that.

I don't either. I can understand on one level they are not very sensitive and it takes big events like 9/11 to see a measureable effect. At midnight in each time zone, the random number generators went out of random stronger in the local time zone, but at the same time there was a world-wide effect and you could watch it march right around the planet as everyone celebrated. It was a special big deal on the millennium.

So it measures not just bad stuff but good stuff too.

Yes, emotionality.

What else would you like to share with us? Usually I have a book to read before an interview, but I didn't in this case.

The Global Coherence Project is the main thing we wanted to talk about. The purposes are to verify the degree to which we could detect earthquakes and volcanoes, but instead of doing it on a local scale as in the past, do it on a global scale. Think of what we are doing as measuring the brain waves and heartbeat of the planet earth. That's metaphoric but not really metaphoric either. If you buy into the Gaia idea that the earth is a living being, we are cells within it, it makes perfect sense.

This work tells us that we are more interconnected in more fundamental ways that we ever thought before. What we do at the individual level matters, such as taking energetic self-responsibility and really managing our emotions and learning to recognize the types of emotions that drain our systems and lead us into incoherence. Learning how to recognize and *shift* those, and take responsibility and choose to run more coherent feelings and emotions through our systems takes us into coherence and renews our system. As more and more people do that, momentum is created to shift from planetary incoherence to coherence. If that interacts with and modulates the earth's field, as good existing evidence suggests does happen, then instead of permeating the planet with stress waves which *everyone* feels—even if they weren't involved, the nervous system still detects the incoherence—we'll get more and more people into coherence, which creates coherence waves.

We behave the way we do much because of conditioning in our lives. People then get on antidepressants or other pharmaceuticals . . . can we avoid that? If you learn how to train your mind with something like this emWave machine, can you override those conditioned experiences?

In many cases absolutely! I can certainly tell you that thousands, many thousands of healthcare professionals are using the HeartMath emotional and restructuring tools to help people overcome anxiety, depression, eating disorders, PTSD . . . we are working with over thirty military hospitals and VAs are now using it for returning soldiers, to help with reintegration issues. The list goes on and on to do exactly what you are saying.

How does someone get an emWave?

The easiest way is to go to the HeartMath website at either *www.heartmath.org* or *www.heartmath.com*. The .org site has more of the research-related information and programs for kids for helping them with taking tests, dealing with anxiety issues, and getting better grades. The .com site features more programs for healthcare professionals or consumers that just want to get one of the books, one of the HeartMath tools, or the emWaves.

It's less than $300 to get one of these to plug into your computer?

There is the emWave PC, which means it works with a PC, and it plugs into the USB port on your computer and it shows your heart rhythms in real time and allows you to see for yourself how changing emotions instantly and dramatically changes your heart rhythm patterns. The heart reflects our feelings. It has games you can play to help teach you to get in a coherent state. There is also the emWave Personal Stress Reliever about the size of an IPod that is portable and does not have to be plugged into a computer and it is under $200. That device is being used by Duke Hospital System, and professional sports players.

I just read ISSSEEM's magazine, and Elizabeth Rauscher was interviewed in it. You and I talked before about the stochastic resonance and afferent signals. Does this work you are doing now relate to that in any way? Will you be able to learn what someone's afferent signals means as it relates to detecting illnesses?

We can already trace the neuro messages going from the heart to the brain. That may sound strange to some people listening but that has been known since the late 1800s. What is surprising to a lot people to learn is that the heart sends far more information to the brain than the brain sends to the heart. We've been so focused on the brain age that we've really forgotten the big picture.

I think that people think that the brain is in charge of everything, but it just interprets, doesn't it?

Exactly, yes. We are finding with the new models and new understanding how most people associate emotion with the heart, and have for centuries. Every major culture on the planet does that naturally. They've been right all along—it is the signals that the heart is sending to the brain that have a lot to do with what we are feeling. Literally, not just metaphorically . . . so the brain is just interpreting those signals.

Let's say I got mad right now for some reason. The heart will send the signal to my brain . . . would measuring that ever be possible?

It's possible now.

They can interpret the signal?

Yes. In fact the emWaves are doing that.

So eventually you should be able to find a certain signal in someone and say, uh-oh, that signal means you are going to get heart disease or . . .

Not so much from the afferent-type stuff we are talking about between the heart and brain. It's both the heart and the brain. They are wired together very uniquely and strongly—more so than any other gland or organ system in the body. When we are talking about predicting disease that is different than when we are talking about emotional experience. We already know that our emotions are reflected in our heart rhythm patterns, and we can measure your heart rhythm patterns, and they are reflective of your emotional state. Not what you are thinking, but what you are *feeling*.

Can you tell us a little bit about other projects you are working on?

Sure. One of the projects we just completed was called the Test Edge National Demonstration Study. It was a huge study funded by the US Department of Education. This was looking at several things, like the relationship between emotional blocks, anxiety, peer issues, etc., and how they affect academic performance.

What did you do?

The main part of the study focused on tenth grade students. We looked at a lot of different elements of their emotional lives . . . certainly their test anxiety, but also their relationships, how many friends they had, the quality of their relationships, and things of that nature. One of the things we focused on was what is the real test anxiety level? The numbers from previous studies before "No Child Left Behind" were all over the map. What we found floored me; I did not expect it. We found that 61 percent of the high school kids are suffering from high levels of test anxiety. One in four suffers very high levels of anxiety that would really interfere with the accuracy to really measure their ability. The anxiety interferes in a major way.

I would have thought they didn't care.

Exactly! Also, we found that a lot of students are really disengaged from the educational process. They are there because they like hanging out with their friends. The students with high anxiety scored about fifteen points lower on average in math and reading than the kids with low levels of test anxiety. Fifteen points is enough to fail you.

Did you intervene?

Yes, there was an intervention component that was taught in English classes two times per weeks for twenty minutes, over three months, called Test Edge which basically taught the students the refocusing technique and emotional shifting techniques that basically has you focus in the area of your heart and breath to the area of the heart to help get your energy pulled out of the area of the heart, then shift emotions to activate a positive feeling—like a feeling of appreciation, for example. The key is to feel the positive feeling, not to just think about it. We installed the emWaves in the schools and the kids really like the emWaves; they really took to the information.

If you had a small machine at home, how do you see results? You see it by a red, blue or green light. Red means you are not coherent, blue means medium coherence, and green means high coherence.

On the computer model you see your heart rhythm going across the screen and the red, blue, and green coherent levels. The main advantage to home computer model is that is has the games to play.

Oh, it really is. The level of anxiety drops significantly, and this is looking at the entire tenth grade population. When we matched the students so they had equal test scores—so we had them academically matched—most of the groups had significant jumps in their actual test scores, which was an amazing finding.

No extra studying, just calming down.

Yes, just giving them the tools to become coherent.

How long did that take?

The intervention was two times per week for twenty minutes over a three-month period. We also found that test anxiety isn't the biggest issue blocking their performance. It's really the wider range, but clearly emotional issues. The students were really clear that they weren't taught tools and didn't know that they could self-regulate and choose what they are feeling. They really appreciated learning that not only they can do that but how to.

I don't think the schools really know about this or understand. I went to my child's school and tried to tell them about this and they had no idea what I was talking about.

We really can regulate our emotions; we have choice.

Have you done some collaborative work with anyone to see the neurotransmitter change?

We have about thirty studies going on right now involving different aspects of HeartMath. One is a collaborative study partnering with Arizona State University; they have a lab that measures all the biochemistry of hormones and things. It will be measuring oxytocin, peptide Y, some of the more exotic stuff in that study.

Do you know Gottfried Kellerman?

No, I don't.

He is at Neurosciences, Inc. I think the website is neurorelief.com. Neurotransmitters are his life and he was so interested in what you are doing.

When I visited you at HeartMath, you asked me all kinds of interesting questions, including one about what happens to plant if you stick them into an electrical socket . . .

We were following up on a lot of Cleve Baxter's work with plants, looking to find ways to make that a more practical and easy thing to do. I was talking about emotions being very real fields, and we don't have instruments that will measure the field directly like we do electric fields and magnetic fields . . . but the types of sensors are biological systems so plants and cells are definitely tuned in to these types of emotions, which is what Cleve Baxter's work has shown.

Can you tell us a little about Baxter and his work?

Cleve Baxter wrote the book, *The Secret Life of Plants* in the 70s or 80s. Cleve is a very interesting guy who invented the lie detector test; the polygraph. He had the idea to hook up his equipment to a plant and found that the plants were sensitive to human emotion. Cleve would sometimes have a plant hooked up to his polygraph and the plant was just as accurate—if not more accurate—in responding when a person was lying than all of the instrumentation.

What did it do?

During negative-type emotions the plants react electrically. It is fairly well researched that plants have electrical signals traveling through them. It is amazing; if I showed you recordings from human nervous systems, when neurons are talking to each other, and their action potential . . . and recordings from plants, you would probably not be able to tell which was which. Even though plants don't have the same type of nervous system that humans do, the electrical signaling being used looks almost identical.

What part of the plant does the signaling, since it doesn't have a brain or heart like we do?

The cells, leaves, stalks and roots are all involved.

Someone also told me that the plants learned by conditioning— that he could do something the first time and they would get upset, but they finally learned that he really wasn't going to hurt them.

That's one of the things that make it difficult to do rigorous scientific protocol. You want to see a very clear cause and effect, stimulus/response, repeatable thing, but plants don't work that way. It takes sincere spontaneous emotion for them to react. So you are exactly right, we see this happen all the time. Someone will walk in and they don't even know the experiment is going on, we have a plant hooked up and you say something that gets them mad or upset and the plants go crazy. If you, say, get mad at the plant it doesn't work because it is not real emotion.

Please tell a potential funder why this is real, why this research important, and why conventional science should listen.

We are all interconnected, and it's very important to learn to take self-responsibility for our energetic system—basically our emotions—and to realize that there really are easy to learn, very practical tools that anyone can learn—a kindergartener or a CEO of a corporation—to care more, appreciate more, and to love more . . . and those emotions create very real fields that, when enough people start doing it, really can create a global shift in our world.

Just for the scientists . . . this science is real and I would imagine it's reproducible.

Absolutely!

I would also imagine that your science is even more rigorous than typical studies.

Well, certainly *as* rigorous. Some things, like our work on intention, is extremely rigorous; way more so than most studies are done, because it is showing results almost unbelievable. We go the extra mile to show the validity and wide-reaching significance of our findings.

CHAPTER 9

Elizabeth Rauscher, Ph.D.

Elizabeth Rauscher was a staff researcher, Theory Group, Lawrence Livermore National Laboratory, professor of physics and general science at John F. Kennedy University of California, research consultant to NASA and Stanford, professor and graduate student advisor with the Department of Physics at the University of Nevada, Reno, served on Congressional OTA, Advisory Committee, delegate and advisor to the United Nations, president of Tecnic Research Laboratories, partner Tecnic Research Laboratory of Apache Junction, Stanford University Grant in astrophysics, Event Horizons. She is the co-founder of the Fundamental Fysiks Group and author of numerous books and hundreds of papers.

Eva: Before we get started, please tell us a little bit about who you are and what it is that you do.

Dr. Rauscher: My background is in nuclear and astrophysics. I have a Bachelor's, Master's, and Ph.D. from the University of California in Berkeley. I worked on the Lawrence Berkeley laboratory staff in both nuclear science and theoretical physics for twenty years. I've had four Navy grants, I've worked on a NASA space shuttle, and I've been a delegate to the UN on long-term energy sources amongst other things including teaching at John F. Kennedy University, the University of Nevada in Reno, the graduate program in physics, and also courses at Berkeley and Stanford.

So how did you get into the study of the science of consciousness?

Well, when I was a child I thought I really wanted to know what the nature of consciousness is. So I started from the very small, the atom, and the very large, the universe, to see where in that whole picture, using the foundation of physical knowledge as the building block towards understanding the nature of consciousness. And that's been my life's endeavor.

What is your definition of consciousness?

That is a very good question, and let me give you an analogy. Forces like the force of gravity, electromagnetic, strong and nuclear, weak force, are defined in terms of particles and waves. But in fact, force itself like f=ma, mass times acceleration, Newton's second law, is not defined except as the properties of force, which are defined in terms of motion and energy and momentum. But the force itself is not defined. I think that's the way it is with consciousness. We can talk about the attributes of consciousness, which I can give you some ideas about. But the actual nature of consciousness itself is self-referential; it's global and universal. And yet we're all coming from different pictures trying to figure out what this fundamental being is.

Alright, that's a very complicated statement. I understand what you're saying, so I want to make sure that my readers understand what you're saying. And you correct me in any way if I'm wrong, please. Are you saying that basically there's one energy and that's all there is and we don't understand how that energy came to be but that we do have one energy, and we all have individual abilities from that energy as well?

I would say yes and no. I think energy is too simplistic a term. Let me give you some of the attributes of the nature of thought and consciousness. Does it have a location? What is its mechanism? What is the mechanism of thought creating reality? Does consciousness has density? What is its dependence on space and time? Does it have a velocity of propagation? Does it have the properties of shape and form? Is it energy or a force of some sort? How does it interact with matter . . . that is mind with matter or consciousness with matter? What is the nature of it in terms of information theory? And why and how is it that our individual consciousnesses are goal oriented. Is the universal consciousness goal-oriented?

Can you answer any of those questions?

I feel from my meditative experience that it does have a density. The further out in the universe that your consciousness goes the less dense it is. I think it has the properties of intuition and intentionality and that thoughts have real consequences because in psychic phenomena people can actually perceive other people's thoughts or animals can perceive human thought. I think it has many of those properties I discussed but I think it's in its own reality. It's all of them combined and more.

Since you are an intuitive, too, I gather, how do you think the original intention came about?

What's the origin of all existence? That's a very good question. I've been looking at that for years. And in general scientists and physicists do not really delve into the nature of consciousness. They sort of deny its existence. They don't seem to realize that no action, no intention, no knowledge, nothing can exist without the action of consciousness as the fundamental nature of their own being. They don't address the issue in many cases, though some are addressing it more in recent years. But one of the things that you had mentioned in the past, and it's true, we don't really have a language yet. We have the neurophysiologists. I'll tell you about a quick meeting in India, in Mumbai. There was the Buddhist, the physicist, and the neurophysiologist. And the neurophysiologist said that consciousness is an epiphenomenon of neural activity. That is the physical comes first and then the consciousness.

The Buddhists and the physicists somehow agree that consciousness may be the primary substance of reality, and then comes matter as a bit condensed out of the physical plane from a higher dimension of all conscious intention and being.

Okay. I think I would agree with the Buddhists and the physicists.

Do you believe we have complete free will?

No, I believe that probably the most likely explanation is we do reincarnate or somehow choose this life, and from a higher perspective, like if you were in a helicopter over a mountain, you could see two cars driving around a curve of the mountain, but they don't know each other's future. They're like at the physical plane until they pass each other. But we have this higher perspective we come into life with and I think the only free will really is accessing the higher spiritual dimensions of what our intention and the purpose of our life is.

Personally I agree with you. But there are going to be many scientists out there that say, why do you think that? Is there some kind of science that led you to believe this, or has it just been your experience?

It's been my personal experience, but I also have formal training in science. And it's also explained in a book from Royal Scientific. I'll tell you more about the book. But what my experience was as a child is why certain things came into my life, like my interest in Nikola Tesla's work to free man from drudgery, so he could think and reason, by developing the electromagnetic power grid. And things like that struck me as very important. One of my relatives said it was to gain and disseminate, the purpose of life was to gain and disseminate knowledge and make the world a better place. So why I would adopt that philosophy is an important result of my past. These incidents seem like the future affecting the past. From the higher perspective it's all happening at once. So you could say I have free will. I can choose vanilla over chocolate ice cream. But why? Why is it you like vanilla? What is the cause of choosing vanilla? In other words, is there a more basic cause than that of just a current free will preferential idea?

So what is your belief, do you think that probable states can be expressions of consciousness and states are consequences of intention?

What do you mean by states?

An event.

I think events may come about both through life plan and carrying out a duty that we have in this existence. And sometimes circumstances shape our being, for example who we're born to and our environment. But within that, how we shape that environment to our meaning of life and our purpose of life is intrinsic to our own being. And that may be access to higher consciousness within ourself. In other words I think that ideas and inspiration and intuition seem to be coming from a higher dimension. As I said, I have worked out a physics formalism to make the compatibility of consciousness consistent with the main body of physics. And that is that we actually have a hyper- dimensional reality which explains the synergy of consciousness with the physical world. The book that I refer to is called *Orbiting the Moons of Pluto: Complex Solutions to the Einstein, Maxwell, Schrodinger, and Dirac Equations (Series on Knots and Everything)*. It's published by World Scientific and written with Richard Amoroso. The key to it is that we have the four-dimensional space of space and time. That is, if we're going to meet someone for pizza we say when and where. So time is really, in Einstein's field, the fourth dimension of space. But then I make that space more complex, into an eight-dimensional space. That allows the non-locality of consciousness both from a spiritual perspective and the ability for our connection with each other across space and time.

Do you believe that intention can manipulate physical reality, matter?

Yes, if intention is directional and strong enough you can affect matter. There are cases of psychic healing. There are cases of psychokenesis, or mind over matter. And my late husband, William van Bise and I did a number of experiments using electronic sensors to see whether people could intentionally affect them during an on-period as opposed to control runs. And we found a highly significant correlation, either when people who intended were about eight miles away or across the country from the laboratory site, which was shielded from ordinary interaction.

Do you believe that, and when I'm asking you if you believe, I'm really talking about from a scientific perspective, because as you know I'm trying to bridge the gap between classical science and the new science of quantum mechanics.

Well, belief is a very interesting issue because it depends on the preponderance of evidence in your own life. And people say you have to have a statistical amount of events to believe in something. Yes that's true, but do you believe in your birth? That's one event. So sometimes it takes only one event to make you believe in something.

Very good point! Never thought about it that way, but that's a good analogy. Many people say that if intention can manipulate reality, why can we not manifest that car that we want in our front yard?

Well, in a sense you can. Through intention, it's possibly easier to intend something good. Like, maybe a method. Since high school I felt we had to get off fossil fuels. So it took a crisis in the oil situation as a forcing function for us to look for alternative, less impacting ways of dealing with energy necessary for crops and a better quality of life. But look at it in a different way. There are forces that we need to pay attention to. And if you intend the car, everything is an exchange in the universe. You have to give to get. Nothing is free. You can't just say one day, "I feel like I deserve that car. It's a Rolls-Royce. Go." There is an action component you have to take on the physical plane to create the circumstances for that intention to come to reality. The universe will give, but you have to work to create that circumstance, to create that in your life. In a certain sense there is sweat equity. You have to deserve it. You have to create the circumstances where you do deserve that gift.

Let's talk about that for a minute. You said you thought that it is easier to create the positive. That brings me to ask a question. What is your definition of mind?

Well, let's distinguish between brain and mind. In general neurophysiologists, biochemists, and so forth defined brain in terms of the physical properties of the various parts: the amygdala, the hypothalamus, the pituitary axis, the pons, and so forth. And a friend of mine wanted to find out the nature of consciousness. So he went with a medical friend of his to dissect cadavers to look for consciousness. And I said you're too late. The consciousness is gone. The guy's dead. And I said it's not so simple. It's not just finding out a gland and its function, which by the way helps us understand what is going on. But consciousness is something that transcends brain. In fact you'd have to say if ghosts are real, and I could tell you some stories about that, if ghosts are real, then they don't have a brain. But they do have actions that mimic what we associate with conscious awareness in some form of existence.

Why then, if you said it's easier to create the positive, are most people run by what I call their "little mind"; you might call it ego. Most people are constantly thinking, I don't want this, I don't want that, I don't like this, I hate that, I can't stand this. They seem to create those things easier. So to me, it seems like it's harder to create the positive because you must stay in the moment to do that and be aware.

Right, number one is what you said, Eva. You have to stay in the now. You have to do both. You have to stay in the now enough. You need to look at the sunsets, the butterflies flying, enjoy the sun, the warmth of the sun and listen to the birds and flowers to perceive your experience of being. You must also plan for the future and really assess and sometimes resolve the past. We live in past, present, and future, and we need to accommodate all of those. But we need to control them. What you call the little mind, the ego, has two sides to it. One is we wouldn't be in a physical body and in this existence . . . in this classroom of life without the ego. If we didn't have an ego we wouldn't eat and do the necessary things for survival. So we need some aspect of ego, but it's the executive part of the frontal lobe and also the general nature of consciousness that we control the role of ego, so ego doesn't run us, ego is a tool for us. The other thing you mentioned is when we say that we don't want A, B, and C, the problem is that psychologists say the "don't" doesn't get heard. So often the fear of what will happen concentrates you on the negative. To concentrate on what you do want in your life and not what you do not want is really a very hard lesson. You need to make a positive affirmation instead of a negative affirmation. Because the universe is listening, but it may not hear the "don't want."

Exactly.

It might hear the "I would like." And I think in a way that's a gentle, positive request. I mean, respect the universe and say, "I would like," and make sure to say thank you.

Do you think ego is a brain function of conditioning? I mean, because our ego is kind of what makes us distinct. Is it a brain function or is it . . . ?

Well, does ego incorporate the aspects of personality? In other words, what really is ego? Is it "I want?" Is it only what I want or does a part of the ego say, I would like to make the world a better place? The ego isn't only negative. My ego also says, yes I would like a green revolution. But one needs to proceed in a positive direction to create that reality. You could say, I don't want to be on a fossil fuel-based reality because wars are waged for oil and the need for oil. But to say, what can I do to create the circumstance of new inventions and new technologies that will replace fossil fuels? That's a positive intention in which you can take a set of action components. I think the ego is related to identity, but identity can be positive elements as well as "I don't want" elements.

Let me see if I can get this thought together. Do you ever wonder, what creates within us? What enforces creativity within us? Would it be emotion (and I'm using emotion as equivalent to voltage) because words are just that, they're just words?

Emotion is part of the biochemistry of the brain, the endorphins, neurotransmitters, dopamine, norepinephrine, etc. But we in western civilization try to train the intellect. In other words, how to do the multiplication tables, but not how to control, have access to, and use the better aspects of emotions. We're told to shut up and sit still in school. And that's not educating the whole being, because we need to educate our physical, our mental, our emotional, and our spiritual states.

I realize that there's no dopamine, norepinephrine, and serotonin floating around in the universe, but something . . . . Let's say that we think a thought, a positive thought and atoms start bumping and oscillating. Information is sent out into the universe and is received back in a kind of revolving door. When I was using the word emotion, I'm really using the word as voltage. What is the voltage behind what pushes things to happen faster or slower? Does that make sense . . . and I understand linguistics is a problem.

Well I think that we really need to develop a new language like you suggested. We need to make means to communicate across disciplines and with people of different backgrounds. The word voltage is kind of like a yes and no. The actual potential difference between cell walls and other aspects of the human body do in fact operate to affect the biochemistry of the body. What I think is, are electromagnetic fields the nature of the fields of consciousness? Yes and no. They're an interface, but they aren't the answer. They aren't what consciousness is. I see it as a field of all being, but also see that it specifically interacts with the physical world with us and all of nature. So I think voltage is too simplistic a term to use.

How do you think consciousness communicates with the brain? How does brain interpret consciousness? Is it through signaling? How does that happen?

I think that at the level of lowest denominator, yes it is signaling and biochemistry, but the actual nature of consciousness, what I consider my personal philosophy, is that consciousness is sort of the global reality. It's like the whole iceberg, and the physical part is ten percent, the tip of the iceberg that we see. We really only notice consciousness as pieces here and there instead of seeing it as a global reality that binds the universe together and allows all communication ultimately to happen not only between individuals but between yourself and your higher being.

Do you believe that matter really exists?

I think so. As the joke goes, I think gravity sucks. Because at this point I'm not able to levitate and I do think the force of gravity exists. In fact, the ancient Greeks had two concepts, gravity and levity. Gravity was formulated by Newton in a very succinct manner, and is really the foundation of modern physics. But I think there's maybe a force of levity, not only a force of attraction. But you might say levity is a force of expanding, and expanding maybe by a positive nature of repulsion. So, I think we have half the picture and not the whole picture.

Do we live in a holographic environment? If we do, that means we live on a level of what I call the irreducible unit, and there's not any matter. So, I guess that's what I'm asking, do we live in a holographic environment and the matter that we see is really just particles stuck so closely together we think that they're mass?

Well, the holographic metaphor of which Karl Pribram and Ed Mitchell and others have looked at is more a metaphor than a model of physical reality. To formulate in detail the nature of existence in terms of a hologram alone is not adequate or not correct. But I think the metaphor gives us an idea of how the pieces connect elements of the whole. I'm actually not particularly into that model. So, the question, does that model contain mass is to me a non sequitur. It doesn't make sense.

I don't understand.

A piece of a holographic representation really contains the whole, but it contains it at a much less resolution. It loses information. From the holographic model I can't see how you could deduce the nature of matter out of it because it's an informational representation.

Is there an irreducible unit?

A fundamental unit like a quark or a gluon?

Yes.

That's a very interesting question. I spent many years in high energy theoretical physics in which the idea was that there was some fundamental unit which actually came from the ancient Greeks with the word atom, which means irreducible. In other words you cannot reduce it beyond the nature of that fundamental unit. And I'm not so sure. I think it might be that we can infinitely divide. And as physics finds smaller and smaller units of existence with the high energy accelerators, it may go on infinitum. Jeffrey Chew sort of suggested that too. He was the director of the theoretical physics group when I was at Lawrence Berkeley National Laboratory. Actually, I don't know the answer, but I suspect it's not going to be a thing where we just say that's it because we go along we keep discovering more. It seems that knowledge is a path, not an end.

I know that you worked with the particle accelerator. How does that thing contribute to humanity?

Excellent question! It's a part of giving us fundamental knowledge, but it isn't going to give us the ultimate answer in my view. Most physicists think it will. So in that sense I differ. I think it's very interesting, very useful, but I'm not sure if you say, ethically and morally, is it worth spending the money on the Large Hadron Collider or the Fermi Lab device, is it worth spending it on that rather than to overcome starvation? The problem is that the roots of starvation have to be met, as well as trying to save individual lives. So it really requires a whole different conceptual framework: how to reduce pain and suffering and enhance the quality of life. As a physicist, of course, I'm interested in accelerator physics, and I'm actually sad that they're talking about closing the Fermi Lab accelerator facility. But on the other hand I can see the argument about spending the money on other areas. So there is a conflict within myself. But I do think that it's part of the purpose of life to gather as much as you can about the various fundamental types of knowledge. Now some of the fundamental types of knowledge are new cures in medicine, a new understanding of the medical modalities, a non-invasive medicine. It's about the nature of man and how man can live with nature and not destroy nature and still have a quality of life. It's about our own spiritual path and the nature of spiritual beings. So it's all of these aspects which can manifest as various ideas within the cultural context.

What did they want to know? What were they hoping the accelerator would find?

Well they wanted to find what's called the Higgs particle, which would describe how matter has its properties. In other words, how is it that a proton, an electron, a neutrino, a pion, a muon, an omega particle, have different quantum numbers, have different properties and different masses, to explain what mass is. What I am saying is there is a drive to try to understand what is the smallest thing in the universe . . . the fundamental building blocks of reality.

Would consciousness, defined as awareness, be in gradients? Everybody has different levels of awareness. I mean, fundamentalism, for example, versus enlightenment, those are gradients of consciousness in my perspective.

I don't know whether I would call it a gradient, but they are distinctly different attitudes, assumptions. Actually our assumptions about what we are studying really colors to a great degree how we interpret what we find because we tend to screen out that which is not consistent with our philosophy. What I find to be the most important thing in my life is to find something that is completely inconsistent—like the nature of psychic phenomena was inconsistent with my assumptions before I studied it. When I found it to be true, I spent three days revising my philosophy to fit the reality. You have to be open-minded and not rush to judgment. In fact, knowledge is an ongoing process. When you grasp things and you think you really know the answer, it's likely you'll have some experience that tells you that you do not. Then you're on to a new adventure to find new information.

When I first had my wake-up call, I woke up the next morning thinking I knew everything because the knowledge had increased so much overnight. You don't know the story, but you will when you come visit me. The more I learn, the more I realize I don't know anything.

I've learned some things in life but I know we are just on the tip of the iceberg. There is so much more to learn.

Tell us a little about what you are doing with HeartMath.

HeartMath was quite interesting. We got in touch a number of years ago, but in more recent years my late husband and I developed a very highly sensitive patent in magnetic field detectors. It detects the changes in the magnetic fields of the earth's ionosphere sphere of resonance and some of this is produced by vibrations within the earth through solar wind activity coming by at charged particles and waves that affect the ionosphere. The HeartMath group commissioned me to do a detector with them, a part of my detector system for the Global Coherence Initiative. They are going to try to support 100 detectors around the world. What is interesting about these detectors is that they detect the fundamental frequencies which we evolved in and relate to our life force. We cannot live a long time without these frequencies, and we would have to artificially generate them to be able to undertake a mission to Mars.

What are those frequencies? What range do they fall within?

They really fall in different ranges all the way from what's called an extremely low frequency radiation to actually seeing cosmic rays up toward the gamma end of the spectrum. We have of course the ultraviolent and infrared and the visible that we notice, particularly the infrared which is seen in the visible, but there is a huge spectrum of frequencies from the extremely low frequency end of the band to the ultra-low frequencies, and the radio frequencies on up to the visual and up into x-rays and gamma rays. We evolved in that environment. If we don't move within that environment we cease to exist without that life-giving set of radiations that we are used to and that we evolved in.

Are they stochastic resonances?

Stochastic comes from the word statistical. No, there are many, many aspects. It ties in with the biochemistry. It actually affects the brain waves, the solar cycle. I have fifty pieces of data showing that certain frequencies of coronal solar ejection actually set their brain waves; so that now we are going into high solar activity, which happens to be about the time we are having freedom marches in the Middle East. Also since there is the interest in 2012, the latest in the Mayan calendar, we are actually going to have high solar activity at about the same time, and some people's expectation and the reality of the influences might be very synergistic and work well together.

I'd like to say something about all the things I've learned and all the stuff I don't know. What is so fantastic is there was a statement by the past head of UC Berkeley that I, Charley Tart, and Jeff Mishlove were wrong because almost everything is known. Now, the interesting thing is that I didn't respond to that because I think we know almost nothing. I consider that fortunate because then we have all kinds of possibilities of changes. I made a list of what I have learned about life. In my life I have been a meditator. Science exists, but I also believe that direct knowing exists. Thoughts are real and have real physical consequences. The past obviously affects the future but I believe there are futures that are so strong in our psychic field that they affect the past through hyper-dimensional geometry. Sometimes it seems it's hard to come by and it does require hard work. We have to dedicate ourselves to the search for peace and knowledge. In many cases what is said to be true may not be and what is said to be myth is true—but you have to sort it out. Truth is in known knowledge and truth is in mystical knowledge. But not everything hypothesized is true. What's called the Blue Pearl of spiritual wisdom is something that you observe after many years of meditation. Whatever it means, I've experienced it and it's real. A kundalini enlightenment exists and is real. I also have seen in my meditations something like the "Eye" which is on the one dollar bill. It is like the eye of God looking at you as an observer so it must represent God. It is a very interesting phenomenon. I've spoken to a few other people that have had that experience. One can do the fire walk even with six-inch flames, not just hot coals.

I'm very afraid of fire and I did it anyway with no problem, so it is possible. One can communicate with animals and plants and one another through mind and consciousness. Kings and Queens wore crowns, but that had to do with the crown chakra. It is giving emphasis that knowledge can come from without if we really listen to the nature of the universe with our fundamental nature. Extreme frequencies and aura frequencies can profoundly affect our biological being but they have to be a very specific wave form, duty cycles, intensities, and other characteristics. I have developed pain reduction systems, cardiac normalizing systems, and other systems using pulsed magnetic fields of very highly specific frequencies intermixes and have a number patents to increase the quality of life. High solar activity affects our brain waves and us. My interpretation is that the sun is talking to us and giving us messages to which we need to listen.

Ghost phenomena are interesting. My late husband and I were driving in this place that was very haunted. I felt like there were a lot of ghosts but I didn't see any. One time we were driving along at dusk and a black ghost floated across in front of our car, and where the eyes would be, looked like open sockets. I could see surprise from the ghost, apparently because we could see it, and then it slowly disappeared. My husband and I both agreed on what we saw in detail. Life after death appears to exist but everyone must find that for themselves. How they think about that, what experiences they've had that lead them to think about that. Also I believe the sun is related to the Son of God. The Sun God is actually a lifegiver. I have had no experiences with extraterrestrials but I don't discount what others say and believe. I just leave those questions open. Be non-judgmental and if you hear something that you don't agree with or don't know, just shelve it and see what happens . . . what evidence supports it and what evidence discredits it. Listen carefully to what people say but don't believe everything. You have to find out what that means within your own living being and conscious state.

CHAPTER 10

Thomas W. Campbell, Jr.

Tom Campbell specialized in experimental nuclear physics and his thesis explored excited states of the NA21 nucleus. He worked for the Department of Defense in the national missile defense program. After retiring formally there, he most recently worked part-time as a consultant for NASA within the Aries I program, and began researching altered states of consciousness with Bob Monroe, author of *Journeys Out Of The Body*, *Far Journeys*, and *The Ultimate Journey*, at Monroe Laboratories in the early 1970s. He is also the author of *My Big Toe (Theory of Everything)*.

Eva: Tom, please would you tell us a little bit about you and what you do?

Tom: I am a physicist and I have written a book called *My Big Toe*. Actually, it's a trilogy. After graduate school, I began my professional career as a physicist doing physics modeling of complex systems for Army technical intelligence. My boss introduced me to *Journeys Out of the Body* by Robert Monroe. A few months later, I was able to meet Robert "Bob" Monroe at his home in Central Virginia. At that time Bob was in the process of putting together a building in which he wanted to build a laboratory to study consciousness. I don't know if your readers are aware of Bob Monroe, but he wrote a set of three books: *Journeys Out of the Body*, *Far Journeys*, and *Ultimate Journey*. Bob was a person who had spontaneous out of body experiences and being a bit of an engineer at heart he studied, played and experimented with them. He wanted to study consciousness because he wanted to make it real; he wanted to make it science. He didn't want to be the strange old guy who had weird unexplainable experiences; he wanted OOBE to be something that could be studied, understood, and taught. I just happened to be at the right place at the right time. He needed some scientists to help him get his lab going and I had just started a job, had the time, and was very interested. I had meditated and consequently understood something about the dimensions of mind, so I jumped at the chance. I told Bob if he would teach me what he knew I would work for him and be his scientist. He agreed and that began a several-decades-long relationship. We began by building equipment and preparing the lab to start researching the nature of consciousness. After two or three years, I and several others working on this project progressed to where we could explore and travel within the larger reality system at will. After OOBE became something we could do whenever we wanted, we started experimenting with its capabilities and limitations as well as trying to develop a way to make the OOBE more accessible to others. I have always approached my experiences as a scientist. I was compelled to verify that OOBE was real and not just a product of my imagination. How does it work? What are the limitations? What does it mean? How does it relate to physical reality? I have been doing this now for about forty-five years and seven or eight years ago I finally figured out how it all worked—physics and metaphysics, the normal and paranormal, science and theology, all came together and were explainable by one overarching scientific theory. To share the information, I wrote the book *My BIG Toe (My Big Picture Theory of Everything)*.

Briefly, what are you doing now?

I am consultant for NASA doing risk analysis for large systems. The job is to make sure that the NASA mission and the astronauts survive . . . what could go wrong and if it does go wrong how we can fix it.

I would imagine that NASA requires an emotionally stable person.

Of course, I live two lives in a way. I don't publicly mix the two a whole lot. When I am at NASA . . . I am a physicist and I make mathematical models and do physics. I don't try to introduce others to the larger consciousness system at work. However, I use my intuitive abilities at work to solve problems—I just don't advertise that advantage to others in the work place.

What is your definition of consciousness so that we can make sure we are on the same page with our discussion?

That is a hard question to explain succinctly because, commonly, people use the word "consciousness" to mean two very different things. Many don't understand this and thus find a single definition to be inherently troublesome. First, there is consciousness as the super system. I call this the larger Consciousness System. This "Big C" consciousness is the only thing that is fundamental. Everything else is virtual, i.e., a derivative of Big C consciousness. Both us individually and our physical reality are derivative of (a subset of) consciousness. To clearly describe what the larger consciousness system (the superset) is by using the concepts, language, and metaphors of the subset (physical reality) is difficult to do with precision. You are asking the little picture subset to describe the big picture superset. I can tell you that the answer to your question probably won't make sense until we've had the chance to talk about some other things and flesh out more about the nature of Big C consciousness. But here goes anyway: Consciousness is information. Consciousness is a digital information field. It is a system of information and information processing that is evolving and aware; it has memory, it processes data and it is self-changing. It is evolving toward its goal of reducing system entropy which equates to becoming love. It would take much more than the time we have to derive these statements with rigorous logic. For that, one must read the books.

I was looking for something like that because a problem exists with a lot of scientists from every field when the word "consciousness" is used. Many think that it is synonymous with awareness and I believe it is so much more than just awareness.

Oh yes! That is the other part of what we call consciousness. We have been talking so far only about Big C Consciousness. Individual awareness (Little C consciousness) is generated by a data-stream from Big C consciousness to a small subset of consciousness I call a Free Will Awareness Unit. This free will awareness unit (FWAU) is what you think of as Eva—the conscious being. You, the FWAU, interpret that data stream as this virtual reality; whereas you, the physical body, are a virtual character in a simulation. Think of your physical existence as being like a character in any interactive multiplayer virtual reality computer game such as "World of Warcraft" or "The Sims," except that the larger consciousness system is the computer and your free will awareness unit is the player (with joy stick and monitor) who gets the data-stream from the game's server. Personal awareness is also a function of your understanding, knowledge, perspective, confidence, fear and ego—all of which develops and changes as you play the game. Game-play provides the opportunity to expand (evolve) the quality of your individual consciousness toward becoming love. Some call this spiritual growth, or simply growing up in the Big Picture. You are a portion of the larger consciousness system and as you evolve, it evolves. All individuated units are netted in what I call the Reality Wide Web. You, as an individuated unit of consciousness, go through a series of "experience packets" wherein you cumulatively evolve the quality of your Little C consciousness. Having many different individuated units of consciousness do this within the virtual reality consciousness evolution trainer we call our universe, represents one of the evolutionary strategies of the larger consciousness system. So you see Big C and Little C consciousness are entirely different but related. All is derivative from The One Big C consciousness

Do you believe that there are gradients in consciousness and if you do what does that mean to you? Everyone that walks around sees the world in a different way, is that due to gradients in consciousness? Why do we all not accept the bigger picture?

That's not a gradient in Big C consciousness; it is a gradient in Little C awareness. We all have different levels of awareness and we are all at different levels and stages of the evolution of our Little C consciousness. The larger consciousness system is evolving. Our particular individual consciousness is evolving. In any individuated evolutionary process there are as many different states or levels as there are individuals. Each of us is on our own evolutionary path. Some are more or less evolved than others as far as their meeting the purpose and function of consciousness (becoming love).

If consciousness is all there is how does it segregate itself? Does that make sense?

Yes, I understand . . . how is it we are all one but yet we are individual is what you are asking.

Yes.

The larger consciousness is an evolving self-modifying, learning, growing information system. We individuated units of consciousness are evolving self-modifying, learning, growing subsets of that system. An information system can petition off parts of itself very easily. It can take part of its informational bits, i.e., memory, processing, purpose, and make a smaller version of itself that is ideal for growing up in the big picture with the help of a virtual reality where it can exercise its free will choices and have the experience and feedback necessary to optimize personal growth. An information system like Big C consciousness can do anything a digital computer can do. It can partition, duplicate, delete, store, modify, and run simulations. Information is just coded bits, ones, and zeroes at the basic level. There are all sorts of ways that a conscious information system can create separate individuated units of consciousness. Now why would a consciousness system want to do that? Consciousness is evolving and evolution comes through experience. Just one monolithic consciousness system experiencing itself doesn't lead to a lot of interesting choices capable of optimally stimulating evolution. To improve its evolutionary progress, consciousness breaks itself into pieces and lets those pieces interact with free will. That is an exceedingly brief description of what we are . . . why we are . . . and who we are.

Do you know how that happens from a scientific perspective?

Yes, I do. The motive force, it's not really a force . . . but the thing that makes changes in consciousness, in this information system, is intent. Conscious intent is what moves data, changes information, and modifies constraints. Change within consciousness is accomplished by and through a low noise focused intent. The larger system is just an evolving system like any system. It must evolve or devolve, evolve or die, thus, it intends, plans, and configures itself to make its evolutionary progress toward lower states of entropy more certain and more efficient. As it turns out, optimal positive evolution (which is accomplished by decreasing system entropy) for a highly interactive set of digital individuated units of consciousness is accomplished when those individuated units interact with a loving intent. The derivation of that fact is probably a half-hour discussion in and of itself. To summarize, spurred on by evolution, Big C consciousness breaks itself into multiple subsets just like biological cells did. Single biological celled entities lowered their system entropy by dividing themselves into multi-celled entities that further divided into various functional parts such as locomotion (legs and feet), sensory and nervous system, etc. They differentiated because their efficiency of function (survivability and procreation) improved with entropy-reducing increased complexity. It is the same with consciousness. It evolved us and it evolved virtual realities for us to grow up in—and it did this to facilitate its own evolution.

Can you discuss how the mass consciousness and individual consciousness differentiate themselves? Why is there that mass consciousness? Does the individual consciousness segregate from the mass consciousness?

Now you are introducing a third kind of consciousness. What we call "collective consciousness" is simply the vector sum of all the individual consciousnesses making up any given group of individuals within our virtual reality. All consciousness within our virtual reality is individual and yet all individuals are also netted together over the Reality Wide Web. This is an information system.

Information is continually exchanged between individuated units of consciousness. Not necessarily at an intellectual level but every consciousness is on the net, much like web pages on the WWW net. Consciousness interacts and communicates in many ways. There is information passing back and forth between everyone on a level that is not physical. These communications influence us. If a mob forms, then one gets a mob consciousness and that tends to descend to the lowest common denominator among all of the people taking part. If you have a group of people together who are interactively growing, learning, and supportive of each other, then that situation tends to pull up the consciousness level of that group toward the highest level present in the group. Group consciousness is not a separate independent consciousness of its own; it is simply a vector sum of its components that is capable of influencing and being influenced by the individual group members.

Do you think that we have free will and please give me your definition of free will.

The answer to that is of course we have free will. We have to have free will because we are conscious. Consciousness and free will are logical necessities for each other. You cannot have consciousness without free will. You cannot have free will without consciousness. I derive that inescapable conclusion in my book if any of your readers would like to see the logical progression and derivation. How do you define free will? I define a thing called decision space. Our decision space is defined as all of the choices we are able to assess at a particular time. Growth is about choices . . . how your intent creates a choice. You have choices to make and your intent will inform that choice. Of all the choices you have in your decision space . . . and that's not necessarily all of the choices there are . . . your decision space is limited if your awareness is limited. You have a limited number of choices (practical choices rather than theoretical choices) that your individual awareness can access and you get to pick one of them. Someone accidentally steps on your toe and one of your choices is to reach out and smack them. Another choice would be to say excuse me, you are on my toe. Another would be to push them off you and another just to stand there and grit your teeth. You have all of these choices as to how you could act and you will pick one based upon how you are, on what is inside of you, on the quality of your consciousness. You have the free will to choose one of those options. How your intent facilitates your choice and thus commits you to some action either helps you along in the evolution of your consciousness, or helps you to de-evolve. It is through these choices, and the feedback that follows, that opportunity is created for Little C consciousness to change itself—to grow up, to evolve, to become love.

Imagine that you are a three-year-old in the back seat of a car and you are strapped into a car seat with a little yellow steering wheel thinking you are driving the car. Source, God, or whatever you want to call it is in the front seat driving the real car. You come upon a stop sign, the playground is on the right and the grocery store is on the left. Source plans on going to the grocery store and you plan on going to the playground. Whose steering wheel is going to work?

Obviously the three-year-old's steering wheel is not going to work. But that has nothing to do with free will.

So my question is do we have free will to place intention or do we really have complete free will?

We have free will to do whatever is in our decision space. Of all those decisions we get to pick one of them. Look at that three-year-old. Making the car go to the right towards the playground was not in his decision space and therefore that decision was not available to him. He could not choose that. Free will does not mean you get to do anything you want. Free will is not equivalent to having a genie in a lamp with unlimited wishes.

So he has free will to place an intention but he is not guaranteed that the intention will occur?

Not if it is not in the decision space. It may not be an available decision. Sure an intention can be placed to go to the playground but that is an "I wish."

You have free will to wish for whatever you want to wish for but when it comes to what you do . . . when you exercise that free will, that is you choosing one of the things in your decision space. That child may decide, when the car goes left instead of right, to scream, holler, and pitch a fit or the child may just say okay, I accept that and go in another direction. Now that is in the child's decision space.

Observation, right? He chooses to observe rather than react. Submission.

It is not a matter of always observe and submit, that is only one choice. One can also scream, be obnoxious and cranky, get angry, make a plan to change the situation, move away from the source of control, never get in the car again without a struggle, spit on the car seat, get a driver license when that choice becomes available, etc. If you are three years old or in prison, "observe and submit" may loom large and your decision space may be relatively small, but, you must deal with whatever you have to deal with at the time until the situation changes or until you make it change.

Does everyone see the same movie?

Does that mean that we all share the same reality?

Do we all see green trees? Is the green the same to everyone? Not color blindness, etc.

Of course not. Our personal physical reality is a virtual reality. It is nothing but data. We take data into our senses and interpret that data to be this physical reality. There is nothing there but data and our interpretation of that data is subjective and personal. That being the case . . . .

Does that mean matter doesn't really exist?

In the larger reality there is no such thing as matter or space, however time does exist in the larger reality, indeed, it is created there. This physical reality doesn't exist as a set of physical objects in and of themselves. Perhaps I shouldn't say mass and space doesn't exist . . . it does exist as data, that is, as virtual space and virtual mass. It exists as information. Mass exists in our virtual reality in the exact same way that mass exists in the computer simulation of a rock rolling downhill. In a computer simulation, mass doesn't exist as physical, heavy, hard stuff—it exists as information. Mass, from the perspective of the larger reality, is data in the computer (larger consciousness system) and it obeys the rule-set that the computer has for dealing with mass (laws of physics). From the viewpoint of a simulated (virtual) character in a simulation, the mass this character interacts with (according to the rule-set) is hard and heavy and takes up space. In summary: from the perspective of the big picture, there is no mass or space; and from the perspective of the little picture, there is the perception of mass and space. Everywhere there is time, although the time in our virtual reality is created especially for our virtual reality by the time increment used in the time loop driving the dynamic simulation.

How does that data exist? Does it exist in frequencies . . . and I hate to use the word frequency but I don't know what other word to use . . . frequencies, impulses, signals, resonance . . . .

No, it doesn't exist as any of those things. The reason that it doesn't is that all of those things are words that define things here in this virtual physical reality-frame which has its own rule-set. The rule-set in this reality frame is physics. Frequency has a meaning here in this reality according to our rule-set. It is something that changes some physical value as a function of time: How many times per second does something happen? That doesn't really translate when you are talking about a non-physical information field. That brings up the point that information itself is non-physical. You can have a book and the book has ink and paper but those things are physical. The content of the book, its meaning and significance, the information is non-physical; it has no mass, and takes up no space. A consciousness is required to get the message. Let's focus on your question again . . . .

How do people in physical reality receive information from consciousness—I call it the ground of all being, that original source—how do we get it? We know brain interprets, but how does it come in as what we perceive it to be?

Our brain actually interprets nothing. Reality is information that is received and then interpreted by a free will awareness unit engaged in a multiplayer reality game simulation. So our reality is generated in the mind (instead of on a monitor with a joystick) of a small subset of Big C consciousness (the FWAU described earlier). What that small subset of Big C consciousness (FWAU) does with the information, how it interprets the data, plays its interactive character, and exercises its free will intent to make choices within the game constitutes its character's Little C consciousness. The body-brain is only a virtual or simulated body-brain. The virtual simulated brain processes, stores, and interprets nothing. The free will awareness unit is the only thing that processes, stores, and interprets information from the data-stream. It is real, and not virtual. Remember we started this interview with the statement that Big C consciousness is the only thing that is fundamental. Unlike "The SIMS," our virtual reality simulation was evolved, not programmed. The simulation (I call it the big digital bang simulation) started with some input constants, a rule-set, and a lot of energy jammed into a hot small ball. When the run button was hit to start the simulation, this ball began to expand and cool . . . and the rest is standard Big Bang theory. What eventually evolved within this simulation (according to the rule-set) was our virtual physical reality with all the things and critters we see around us including humans. The virtual body-brain represents the constraints placed on human characters according to the rule-set. That is all. The virtual simulated brain processes, stores, and interprets nothing, it serves only as constraints. We can't jump twenty feet in the air or learn differential equations in three minutes because the rule-set doesn't support it. If our virtual character gets hit in the head and ends up with brain damage, which simply adds the additional appropriate constraint (according to the rule-set) to that character's functioning. The data stream sent to the FWAU defines all the information that our virtual character would get from its virtual senses, just like the data stream sent to your computer monitor defines all the information that your virtual "Sims" character would get from its virtual senses. The idea that consciousness communicates information to our brain and that our brain processes that information is a decent metaphor but not correct. Nor does our brain communicate with other brains in some unknown way. All the action is accomplished in consciousness by the FWAU interacting with the data stream generated by the larger consciousness system that defines the interactive multiplayer consciousness evolution trainer we call physical reality. Also all individuated units of consciousness (within any reality-frame) are netted and can communicate by exchanging data. Data links are opened and closed through focused intent within a low noise environment (no fear, no ego).

Why is it that there are people with fundamental perspectives who say, for example, "it is THIS way and it cannot be any other way," and then a few years down the road they begin to know there is something more and one day they have an epiphany and their awareness suddenly expands?

First of all that fundamentalism ("fundamental perspectives") is a product of belief. Belief is a limiter. A belief blocks your ability to know something new that conflicts with that belief. A belief becomes a trap that tends to lock us in to a particular perspective. Belief is typically entangled with our fear and ego. Get over a fear, or let go of some ego, and suddenly new information, that was always there but somehow invisible, becomes available and accessible. We are a part of this consciousness system that is trying to evolve and we are part of that evolutionary process. The consciousness system wants us to succeed—our success is its success. It bumps and nudges us to evolve, grow and become more loving.

Is there some science as to why that happens? For example when Edgar Mitchell came back from the moon he had a spontaneous epiphany . . . is there some science that supports why that happens?

The science that supports it is really the understanding of what and why we are here and how we interact with the larger consciousness system. If you understand those things then you know exactly why you go boom . . . this is part of your evolution, this is why you are here . . . to grow up and get the bigger picture and not be trapped in beliefs. Physical reality is a learning lab and sometimes it takes a bump to have things fall together and sometimes that bump is that the system does something that forces you to realize that reality is bigger than just the physical.

Do you know what it is within that system that is bumping?

It is the innate drive to evolve.

Is it related to entropy?

Yes, the innate drive to evolve can be stated as the innate drive to decrease the entropy of our individual unit of consciousness, which also decreases the entropy of the larger system. I use entropy as a physics term, but basically that means to grow the system in its knowledge and organization . . . to make the system better. What that translates to is low entropy consciousness, which is love. We are growing towards love, kindness, and caring. That is how an information system like consciousness evolves . . . towards lower entropy. Lower entropy implies more organization, i.e., more usable and functional information.

I would like to read something from your book about how to change your "movie" if you don't like it . . ."the organizational energy that created the peak in the first place must first be dissipated in order to remove or reduce that event expectation value." What does that mean from a scientific perspective? I want people to understand that there is scientific evidence that they really can change their reality.

First you have to understand the way consciousness works. Here is a very quick overview: to really understand what I am saying and how it works, one should read the books or watch the videos on YouTube. Consciousness has a process by which it generates these virtual realities we have been speaking of and part of that process is the generation of a probable future database. That is a database that contains all of the things that we could possibly do during the next delta-t and the probability that we will do them. There are also historical databases that are part of the process of generating virtual reality: Everything that did happen in the virtual reality and everything that could have happened but didn't (along with the probability of it happening). Fact is, one can affect the probability of a possible future event by using a low-noise focused intent. With your mind you can make a future possibility (a potential happening) more or less probable (more or less likely to happen) if you focus your intent on it. In a virtual reality, all future states remain un-rendered into the physical reality until some FWAU requires the data. Free will makes choices only in the present and we do not have to choose what has been calculated as most probable. For example, let's say you have a lump someplace and it is a probable cancerous tumor. You can lower the likelihood of that tumor being cancerous for yourself (or for another) by changing the probabilities of it being cancerous with your intent. Intent modifies the probabilities within the probable future database. What I am telling you is the same thing that quantum mechanics talks about when they say that particles are probability distributions. Once you make a measurement you get an answer. The measurement making information available within our virtual physical reality collapses the wave function to a "physical" state. That is the way all of our virtual reality works—the principles of quantum mechanics do not just apply to tiny subatomic particles. Quantum physics is just one specific application of a more general set of principles. So, the short answer is, "Yes": for any event there is a statistical distribution within the mechanism that generates our virtual reality that gives the probability of what is likely to happen next, and you can influence that likelihood any time before the measurement is made and collapses the probability into an actuality within our virtual physical reality. There is much more to this discussion than we have time for. *My Big Toe* actually not only explains metaphysics but also solves the outstanding big mysteries of science as well. It explains quantum physics theory and results, why the speed of light sets an upper speed limit for mass traveling though our virtual reality, the placebo effect, and in general how mind and matter are entangled. Take a look at "twcjr44" YouTube channel for more information.

I have noticed in the past couple of months while I am doing something that a fleeting thought will randomly run through very, very quickly . . . it just flies by and if I didn't know what I know, I would let it go. However I've started paying attention to that fleeting thought and following up on it . . . go check this file, go do this or go do that . . . . and I've noticed that if I catch that fleeting millisecond thought and act on it, every single time it has been right. The information contained in that thought will usually be valid for two or three days. I wonder if that is the window of free will?

There is no window on free will. Free will is your freedom to choose from the choices you have. What you are experiencing with those fleeting thoughts is that you are in communication, as is everyone all of the time, with the larger system. You have access to those databases I was just talking about. Also, the system wants us to succeed in our effort to grow up in the big picture so it is trying to help us. One of the ways it interacts with you and lets you know that there is a larger reality and helps you see bigger pictures is by making this information available to you. You have the sensitivity to actually bring it up into your intellect. Everybody has access to that kind of information but often they don't have the clarity and low noise consciousness or are not in tune enough to actually translate it into their intellect. You do and you have learned to pay attention to it. I have too. I get the same sort of things. We call that intuition. Intuition is just a metaphor for one of your interfaces with the larger consciousness system. It is not a matter of a window on free will; rather it is an opportunity of free will choice. Free will does not come and go. The three-year-old didn't have a choice to go right—making the car go right or left was in his mom's decision space but not in his—however, he did have a choice as to whether to cry about it or not. If you pay attention you will notice that the system is always offering you useful information and nudging you in the right direction.

How does death fit into the picture of consciousness?

There is no such thing as death in the "real world," that is, in the big picture painted by consciousness. Death in opposition to life is an artifact of our virtual reality—a logical consequence of the rule-set that defines this virtual reality trainer. Within a virtual reality both "dead" and "alive" are both impossible. It's just a simulation—information and rules. However, you can be alive within consciousness. Your FWAU and individuated unit of consciousness is "alive" when it is being played in some virtual reality. The larger consciousness system is alive always. Consciousness evolves, and death can only come from persistent de-evolution. You join the awareness of this virtual physical reality and you are alive in this reality. When you leave this virtual reality frame, your character is dead within this reality, but you are still consciousness fully alive within another virtual reality. You just no longer participate into this virtual reality game as that particular character. There is no such thing as death; there are only transitions between reality-frames . . . a connection to a different data stream. You are virtually alive in this physical reality or you are virtually dead. Both are just local perspectives from inside the simulation.

The body just drops away, everything else is still there.

That is correct.

About the Author

Eva Herr has become one of the most respected and popular talk show hostesses on Internet radio via her show, "The Infinite Consciousness," on BBS Radio. For years she has had the opportunity to engage the minds of today's top thinkers in the fields of science and consciousness, as well as on holistic, functional, ortho-molecular, and alternative medicine resources for diseases of the mind and body. A list of her past interviews reads like a "who's who" of luminaries throughout the world. She herself has also been a guest on many radio shows, has spoken at conferences, and has appeared in movies and documentaries, and on television. She was a member of the steering committee for the Human Health Project and she currently sits on the board of directors for the Alliance for Addiction Solutions. She also writes a regular column in several magazines.

Eva is a certified holistic counselor and a world-renowned medical intuitive; as such, she works with clients using her encyclo-pedic knowledge of alternative/holistic health remedies, as well as helping people understand how our mind and body work together, enabling them to better understand and educate themselves, and providing hope through alternative solutions for illnesses they were unable to resolve through traditional allopathic medicine.

Eva currently lives in the Appalachian Mountains of North Georgia, and can be reached via her website, www.evaherr.com.

.

Related Titles

If you enjoyed *Consciousness*, you may also enjoy other Rainbow Ridge titles. Read more about them at *www.rainbowridgebooks.com*

The Cosmic Internet: Explanations from the Other Side
by Frank DeMarco

Conversations with Jesus: An Intimate Journey
by Alexis Eldridge

Dialogue with the Devil: Enlightenment for the Unwilling
by Yves Patak

The Divine Mother Speaks: The Healing of the Human Heart
by Rashmi Khilnani

Difficult People: A Gateway to Enlightenment
by Lisette Larkins

When Do I See God: Finding the Path to Heaven
by Jeff Ianniello

Dance of the Electric Hummingbird
by Patricia Walker

Coming Full Circle: Ancient Teachings for a Modern World
by Lynn Andrews

Thank Your Wicked Parents
by Richard Bach

Afterlife Conversations with Hemingway:
A Dialogue on His Life, His Work, and the Myth
by Frank DeMarco

The Buddha Speaks: To the Buddha Nature Within
by Rashmi Khilnani

Jesusgate: A History of Concealment Unraveled
by Ernie Bringas

Messiah's Handbook: Reminders for the Advanced Soul
by Richard Bach

Blue Sky, White Clouds by Eliezer Sobel

Rainbow Ridge Books publishes spiritual and metaphysical titles, and is distributed by Square One Publishers in Garden City Park, New York.

To contact authors and editors, peruse our titles, and see submission guidelines,please visit our website at *www.rainbowridgebooks.com.*

For orders and catalogs, please call toll-free: (877) 900-BOOK.